A SOUL'S OASIS

A SOUL'S OASIS

A Woman's Transformational Journey
Through Tragic Life Events

A Memoir

By

Carrie Cunningham

authorHOUSE®

AuthorHouse™
1663 Liberty Drive
Bloomington, IN 47403
www.authorhouse.com
Phone: 1-800-839-8640

Published by AuthorHouse   02/14/2012

ISBN: 978-1-4685-5087-0 (sc)
ISBN: 978-1-4685-5086-3 (e)

CONTENTS

ACKNOWLEDGEMENTS vii

PROLOGUE ix

THE BEGINNING OF THE END.................................1

THE DILEMMA..5

MY BEGINNINGS...10

MOVING FORWARD 15

MY STORY BEGINS 21

FINDING A HOME 26

BLOOD, SWEAT AND FEARS 31

MORE BLOOD, SWEAT AND FEARS 37

THE UPHILL CLIMB..43

REMINISCING..50

STILL CLIMBING 54

NOT SO SWEET SIXTEEN 62

THE VIEW AT THE TOP.......................................66

THE UNRAVELING..71

TOUCHED BY AN ANGEL....................................75

LETTER TO MARK...80

THE COLLAPSE...85

INNER JOURNEY 90

THE JOURNEY CONTINUES 95

LOOKING BACK 100

SOULMATES 106

BITTERSWEET EMBRACE 111

LETTERS TO GRANDMA 116

COUPON QUEEN 122

MORE EMBRACES 127

ANYTHING'S POSSIBLE..131

NEW TRADITIONS 135

SANTA'S PET MAIL EXPRESS...138

FINDING MY WAY 142

SAYING GOODBYE 148

WANNA KARAOKE? 154

OPENING MY VOICE 159

CAUGHT BY SURPRISE..164

THE AWAKENING..170

REFLECTIONS 172

EPILOGUE 175

ABOUT THE AUTHOR..179

ACKNOWLEDGEMENTS

Thank you to Lyn Roberts, editor, and Ellen Barrons, proofreader, for pushing me to a higher level than I could have gone by myself.

Thank you to my daughters Erin and Kayla for supporting and encouraging me to tell my story.

Thank you Gary, for giving me the freedom to pursue my dream, and for your patience while I wrote and revised for many long hours.

Thank you to all my family and friends that participated in reading early drafts and sharing their feedback.

PROLOGUE

Gasping for air, I yearned for a way out. If only the stairs had been underneath me, guiding me to the surface, enabling me to stay afloat. But they were on the other side of the pool, far out of my reach. No one lent a hand. I needed to be rescued. Words from the Beatle's song, "Help," flashed into my mind. The words "Help, I need somebody, Help me get my feet back on the ground," danced in my head.

There was no way to find my footing, as there was water above, surrounding me, to a depth of twelve feet. There was no lending hand either, only a brutal one, forcing deeper and deeper descent into the icy pool.

This became the pivotal moment of my life.

It was during the summer of my eighth year that I took a courageous plunge, as I dutifully took swimming lessons in the icy waters of the city pool. That summer became particularly memorable because it marked the event that would stay with me forever. I was not an especially good swimmer. I don't remember failing, yet it could be one of those many images that managed to become buried within the cobwebs of time. I do remember, however, being deathly afraid of swimming underwater. I also have a vivid memory of the unforgiving instructor, who seemed to be lacking even one ounce of compassion. He took humiliation to a level I had not yet understood in my young life.

Test day arrived, and he marched us to the other side of the pool where the diving board stood as a reminder of the dangers lurking beneath. The darkly tanned, broad-shouldered instructor with massively rippled muscles, was a sharp contrast to my skinny frame. As he jumped into the water, resurfaced and met me face to face, his size intimated me. Here we were going to the forbidden deep end, a place I had never been before.

My turn to leap. We were to tread water for a number of seconds, although it felt like minutes, before the time ended. Treading with my thin legs and torso took its toll, but I complied. Then he said those awful words, "bob down into the water." Being the all-powerful adult, and I the lowly child, I felt I had no recourse, so I obeyed. I bobbed. It apparently did not please him, because he began pushing me underwater, mercilessly, each time my head barely reaching the surface. I gasped for air each time I resurfaced. With each plunge, I sank deeper into the water, gasping as if it were my last breath.

This ritual seemed to go on forever, until I choked, and became overtaken by silent screams. The instructor didn't seem to notice, or care. In fact he laughed, booming, "What a baby!" Whatever fear I previously had of the underwater world, was now forever cemented into the highway of my future. I had just experienced what I would experience for much of my adult life- gasping for air.

It is in telling our stories that we heal ourselves, and heal others, giving us courage and empowering us to move forward. This is my desire in telling my own story. It is not only healing for me but for others, who might see themselves and find healing as well.

CHAPTER 1

THE BEGINNING OF THE END

My eyes flew open as if awakened from a deep slumber of another time and place. Darkness still lingered with only a ribbon of light streaming from the window. Beads of sweat stood in rows on my forehead. Too afraid to move, my dampened palms were frozen in place. My heart raced with palpitations that formed short, quick breaths. Utter fear paralyzed my whole being. Resisting the urge to descend back into the dream, my eyes would not stay open.

It felt so real.

Looking up, I surveyed a steep staircase, with as many as thirty steps. They were a deep ruddy brown, and of narrow depth, although they were wide. My vision was faint as shadows of darkness billowed around me. That's how I felt, like a shadow, with the life drained out of me. Each footstep took tremendous exertion. In fact, it consumed every bit of strength and energy that I had. A thick, wooden rail became my only leverage. Sweat rained down my face, and as I remembered, I felt my own sweat released into a trickle that landed on my pillow.

Leaning against my left side was a male figure, with his head weighing heavily on my shoulder. He barely lifted his feet, but instead, relied primarily upon using me as leverage to drag him up the steep slope. There was no movement without the burdensome figure pressing on me. In fact, I no longer had a life, without this appendage glued to my side. *Who was this?!* I felt excruciating pain. I knew my destination was to reach the top of the stairs. There was no other way.

As I continued to struggle forward, an overpowering force moved against me, causing me intense anguish. I made little progress. The task felt hopeless. I kept pushing back at the force. I wasn't going to let anything stop me. There was no other option but to keep climbing the stairs.

Mentally, I kept climbing. Emotionally, I felt more and more oppressed by the figure weighing on me. I held onto the rail for dear life. It was all I had. Sobs of despair overtook my every breathing cell. The experience seemed to last forever. *Did the stairs have an end to them?* Finally, I reached the top. I was alone, no longer was the figure present. Instead, I was standing with my arms outstretched. I felt joyful. The long climb was over.

I started to cry.

What did this all mean?!! I was bewildered.

My dream continued.

My feet were planted near the bottom of the stairs. I knew it had been me. I didn't know who the male figure was. I looked up, knowing that in reality, my journey had not yet begun.

I forced myself awake. I was only able to move my eyes.

They scanned the room looking for clues, anything to capture this unexplained terror that was resonating through me. I became aware of my sister's soft breaths on the bunk bed above me. What I had just experienced certainly was not disrupting her sleep. Aah, my sister Gina, the sweet baby in the family. I was surprised when she agreed to be my college roommate. We shared bedrooms while growing up, with an on-going battle of wills, which portrayed itself in light-flickering, furniture-moving, and sour-faced pouts of silence. The height of separation was in hanging a blanket on a rope between our beds, creating an illusion of aloneness. Yet, here we were as college roomies. Funny, we still do the "light flickering," but other things have subsided. A sudden snort jolted me to the present moment, and the engulfing terror.

The eerie shadows revealed themselves to be the scant furnishings in the room. Desks with textbooks lined in rows, waiting to be opened. Dressers with items draped over the half-opened drawers, ready for easy dressing. A long closet showed nothing had been touched. We always kept it closed. We always locked our door. No one, or nothing, had entered our room. Why then, did I feel so scared?

Rarely were there intrusions in this secluded, peaceful town in Illinois. In fact, there wasn't much more than the college here. A single theater, drugstore, and grocery store lined Main Street. One or two hotels and a gas station were farther outside town. Oh, and the infamous Ben's Burgers was a savored attraction for many. Odorous drifts of the dairy farm could be caught when the wind blew south, and sometimes we could hear ferry horns from the Mississippi, if we really strained.

Gina had always been a bouncy blonde. As she'd gotten older her hair turned to a streaked sandy rendition of her younger self. The combination of her sandy hair, green eyes and speckled freckles across her nose, gave her a country image, making a statement that she belonged here. We were both about 5'4" tall, but my thin brown hair, blue eyes, and massively freckled face was a sharp contrast to her coloring. We were definitely sisters, however, in our manner and preferences.

It was 1976, my junior year in college.

Captain and Tennille were singing, "Love Will Keep Us Together," and we hadn't even found it yet! In our small private high school, we hadn't been allowed to wear blue jeans, but here in this college town, it was "anything goes." We lounged in our bell-bottom blue jeans every chance we got. We'd spent hours decorating the hems with brightly colored fabrics before heading for college in the fall.

Quaint was only one endearing term I would use to describe this town where I spent four of the most important years of my life. Indelible fond memories are forever glued to my soul.

The sound of a slamming door in the hallway jolted Gina awake. She leapt from her top bunk to grasp a cup of water. As she did so, she peered over in my direction. Startled, she asked, "Carrie, why are you crying?"

The sound of her voice brought me back to the dream.

As I struggled to find words for what I had just experienced, my body took on new sensations. The terror lifted, still leaving behind the fear, but adding a heightened sense of perception that sent surges of tingles through me that seemed to say, "Listen. This is real. There is truth in this dream." *But what was the truth? What parts were real? How did I make sense of it?*

These questions would haunt me in the days ahead, disrupting my peace.

CHAPTER 2

THE DILEMMA

My hand reached over to turn off the alarm, to stop the incessant buzzing in my head. Why wasn't it turning off, I thought. After several attempts, I roused enough to be aware that the piercing sounds were coming from the hallway, and not my alarm. As my mind tried to make sense of the situation, I looked towards my roommate Mary's bed. Freshman year had just begun. Mary hailed from Michigan State and every bit a year older than me. She had readily taken to mothering me. Heaven knows I needed it. She looked out for me. I probably needed that too.

Mary was nowhere to be seen, and morning had clearly not yet arrived, even though the hall light glimmered. Hmm, that's strange, I observed. With that, I decided to go look for her. As I entered the hallway I became aware that there was no one else in sight. I kept walking. When I reached the top of the wide staircase at the end of the hall, I gazed out onto the building entryway. There were the girls from the entire dorm, standing, pointing, and laughing at me. Of course, they were donned in their pajamas too.

The homey old brick building would be my freshman dorm, with carpet and stand alone floor furnaces. There were even sinks in every room. A few years later, the dorm Gina and I shared would be very different, where we had vinyl flooring and newer central heating.

Mary came back inside, to my rescue. She guided me to the fire escape slide. As we walked, she explained that the boys had pulled the alarm, to lure the girls outside.

"They're probably hiding in the bushes, watching us," she mused.

"Sounds like something the boys would do," I agreed.

"You know, if you hadn't gone to bed so late, maybe you could have gotten up when the alarm first went off," she commented.

Mary the guardian, once again, looking out for me. She was right. She observed that I had developed the habit of staying up really late, and then couldn't get up for class, let alone anything else. I had always been a heavy sleeper so it usually took a herd of wild elephants to wake me.

When we made it down the slide, the girls started clapping. *How embarrassing. The last one out.*

During my first year in college, I spent a lot of time going out with boys. I didn't make the 4.0 I had kept in high school, although I still kept up a pretty good GPA. Boys accompanied me whenever I wasn't studying or writing a paper. Mary made jokes about my popularity. She also noticed my flightiness. "Just like a bird," she had laughed, "unable to come in for a landing." She had once compared me to Goldie Hawn, not for her looks, but for her capricious image. It must have been my immaturity.

While Mary and I were roomies, we talked marriage, among other topics. We were equally focused on going about the business of getting a man, even though we had different strategies. She had her eye on one man in particular.

I told her the story of my grandmother, who, at a very young age, began praying about who she would one day marry. Grandmother held the belief that we each have one person best suited to be our companion in life. She told of a dream where she saw a man get off at a bus stop. He was tall and blonde, and not the preconceived image she'd had of dark and handsome. But as she experienced her dream, she became aware that this blonde man she'd pictured, would be her husband. In a matter of a few weeks, she met the man from the dream. They ended up marrying.

I clung to that idea. At a very young age, I began praying about who I would marry. My own parents were still together, and although it had been rocky for them at times, they seemed to love each other very much. The idea of being married for a lifetime scared me and yet I was still driven to seek eternal bliss with "the one." This seemed to be the biggest burning question in my young life. Who was the right one?! God, please tell me!

Mary felt she got her answer and left school at the end of the year to get married.

That summer I saw Rick at summer camp in Iowa. He was the same Rick I'd met at camp in high school, but suddenly he looked more intriguing. Gina was actually attracted to him initially, but never openly acknowledged it. She spoke of him as a fun friend. I interpreted it to mean he was "open game," and I became a flirt with a mission. I think I hurt Gina. I regretted that, but we never openly discussed it. From time to time, I felt nudges of guilt, even though she would deny her interest in him. I secretly admired her creativity and carefree spirit, a sharp contrast to my more introverted, yet also fun nature.

Rick and I just seemed to belong together, with our freckles and blue eyes. Few could top our quick-witted banter. So when he began attending the same college in Illinois, dating steadily became an easy transition. I had grown tired, finally, of dating multiple suitors, without having the closeness or security of any one of them. Rick proved to be attentive and I found that I didn't even miss the abundance of phone calls, flowers, and compliments I had grown accustomed to.

Rick and I spent the next three years together, huddled close. The cold Illinois winters eased us into overcoming our shyness. Rick became an anchor for my wind-blown sails. He became the voice of reason when I needed it. He became my ever-constant companion. I no longer had to make decisions about whom I would be with, or how my time would be spent. I knew I would be with Rick.

He seemed like a perfect companion in every sense of the word. Too perfect; I wanted to ruffle his feathers, to check his authenticity. I'd never seen him angry, and he seemed to tolerate a lot from me. *Would that shift at some point, and he would "let it all out?"* This notion permeated my thoughts at times, and contributed to a restlessness I felt deep within. The restlessness said, *I want adventure, I want challenges, and I'm not sure if I want neat and tidy, with everything laid out before me.* Rick was predictable. He would always live near his family. I knew that. He would have steady, secure employment. I knew that too. I also felt his ambitions would not be far-reaching.

These thoughts contributed to lingering doubts that never touched the surface for long.

Whenever they tried to emerge, I quickly buried them. A large part of me wanted life to fit together neatly, and that bigger part of me wanted Rick. We became engaged in 1976, my senior year of college.

It seemed only right that I would have the clarity that my grandmother had in her dream. I continued praying.

Rick and I were in the college library studying, when I ventured downstairs to the basement to go the bathroom. Another sparse Sunday evening, so there were very few others keeping us company. As I walked downstairs, my eyes caught glimpses of two boys sitting in the corner of the room, opposite the bathroom door. As I entered, I noticed their eyes following me. Inside the bathroom I walked through a lounge area, then entered a second door where a long wall of narrow stalls greeted me. Just as I pulled down my pants, the lights turned off.

The room went pitch black. My heart stopped. Desperately I prayed, *"God help me!"* The answer came back loudly in my head, *"Get out!"* Without hesitation, I yanked up my pants and in another swooping motion grabbed the handle of the stall door. What had previously taken five or six steps was now taking only one, to reach the next door. In spite of the lack of light, my hand knew just where to land on the knob. In another giant leap, I arrived back at the entrance door. Swinging it open, one of the boys faced me with his mouth hanging open, eyes wide, and stunned, "C-could you go get my girlfriend's scarf?" as he pointed back inside.

"Get it yourself!" I gushed, as I pushed my way past.

I didn't walk up the stairs. I RAN, skipping steps as I went. My mind raced and my heart throbbed so loudly it was all encompassing. *The other boy must have been inside the bathroom. They were going to rape me.* I knew it without even a moment of doubt.

By the time I climbed the two flights back up to Rick, I visibly shook.

"Rick," I stammered, "Someone just tried to corner me in the bathroom. I think he was going to rape me."

"What?!" Rick refuted, "That's kind of a stretch, isn't it?"

"I know it. I could feel it, Rick," I pushed back.

Rick laughed, "That's crazy."

I was terrified. Rick was laughing, reeling in the pain of the little eight year old at the swimming pool with the heartless instructor.

That scared me more. I needed Rick, and he deserted me.

In that moment, the wall of doubt grew a wider crack. The gnawing questions lurking beneath were surfacing, and now swimming in the murky swamp of my future. We didn't talk about it much after that, but I never forgot, not only what happened, but Rick's reaction. I never told anyone. I feared the boys would try it again, another time, another place.

I needed Rick's emotional support. When he didn't support me in the moment I needed it most, it terrified me. In spite of the bathroom incident, what I didn't realize about Rick at the time was that he was one of the most loving people I would ever know. When I felt it, I didn't feel deserving of it. Why?

It just seemed unbelievable. How could this person who abandoned me emotionally in a desperate moment, also be loving?

He reflected his parents wishes for his life and I wanted him to separate himself and strongly say, "This is who I am, and yes, I choose you. I love you and am willing to blend my life with yours," whatever that meant.

I never gave him that chance. We remained engaged through college, but soon after graduation, I broke our engagement. My restlessness and fear of the future overshadowed my desire to be married. The thought continued to plague me, *Was he the man in the dream?* I didn't want a life of pain and struggle such as the dream portrayed. I didn't have any clear answers.

I was only twenty-one.

It would be many years before I would understand.

CHAPTER 3

MY BEGINNINGS

It was 1966. I was eleven years old.

The soft fuzz of the blanket underneath me was a sensation I dearly loved. The blanket, along with the cool feel of the grass between my fingers and toes, contributed to my outdoor haven. Never mind the chiggers and other land-held critters lying in wait to nibble on me. There was a rare serenity that drew me to lie and gaze on many a star-filled sky on summer evenings. The heat of the Iowa day lingered with less humidity at this time of evening. Frequently, the touch of a gentle breeze heightened the sensations that were already ripe with wonder. The vast, clear, sparkling sky permeated me with the awareness of my existence inside a world that was beyond my comprehension. The arousal awakened me to the reality of my life as a form that encompassed more than my body.

Funny, I am always drawn to nature. Gina and Karen, my neighbor and best friend, always wanted to play dolls. *I'd rather grind cornmeal, or gaze at the stars.* I was just naturally drawn to connect with living things, as well as people. One of my favorite spots was under the big willow tree. I loved the long slender branches as they whipped through the wind. It felt natural to grind cornmeal on the small cement slab underneath the willow. The cement must have been the cover to one of the pipes running from the house, located nearby.

That's where I could be found, while Gina and Karen were playing Barbies.

If I wasn't grinding cornmeal, pretending I lived back in the 1800's, I could be found reading a book. In our small town, it was an easy walk downtown where the cherished library held new adventures to be devoured. *The Little House on the Prairie* series was my favorite. There were few Nancy Drew books that I left untouched as well.

"Carrie!" It was my mother. She didn't like me to be outside by myself in the dark for long.

"Coming, Mom!" I answered back. It was a short walk to the back door, so I was reluctant to get up before I had to.

"Carrie, don't make me come out there after you!" She hollered again.

Her tone signaled urgency. My lingering moments were gone. Time to eat, and waiting meant I risked missing dinner.

As I sat down to eat, I noticed there were yellow flowers on top of my salad. *Those were dandelions*! "Hey, what's going on?" I questioned.

"Well, you're always being Yule Gibbons, wanting to eat healthy. Dandelions are healthy," my dad chuckled. "Your brother's the one who put them on your salad."

"Hey," I pouted, as I glanced over at my brother David, and sister Gina. Both of them were laughing. My mom joined in with the others. I took it good-naturedly. My reputation stuck as the health conscious one in the family. I frequently asked my mom to buy whole wheat bread, instead of white. It just *felt* healthier.

We had lots of fun in our family. My favorite time of year—going camping in the summer in Wyoming or Colorado. We were loaded into our family vehicle (usually a station wagon), and drove the long drive to the mountains. We had a family "pee jar." Dad didn't like stopping, so when we had to go, we took turns crouching under a blanket in the back seat, while trying to handle the jar so that we not only hit inside it, but also so that it didn't spill! Usually we were not 100% successful, so the air was permeated with a twinge of urine odor that accompanied our trips.

By the time we reached our destination, the sky hovered in darkness so that Dad and David were left with the task of setting up the tent.

There were lots of mumbled utterances along with a few yells during these moments. I don't think that part created too much fun! The funniest thing, I think, was watching Mom and Dad zip themselves up together, inside sleeping bags that were attached. When one of them had to go to the bathroom, they laughed and squirmed like caterpillars around the tent, trying to get loose from the bag.

One time, a squirrel got inside our tent and made its way inside a paper bag. We spent a long time speculating about the noise, and where it might be coming from. Finally, we figured it out and set the varmint free.

We did lots of hiking up and down mountain trails, around waterfalls, through many splendid picturesque views. David, Gina and I would race ahead of Mom and Dad and hide behind trees, then jump out and scare them when they approached.

We explored.

We laughed.

We bonded.

We had campfires.

Then we did it all over again. These were some of the best times we had as a family.

Halloween was another time our family had lots of fun. We always carved a pumpkin. Dad would set it on the fireplace ledge and light it. In fact, I think there were two pumpkins! Later, when Gina and I were getting ready to go to sleep, Dad would sneak in the room, crawling on the floor and thrust the pumpkin out saying, "Rawrrr . . ." trying to scare us. We always giggled and were startled, even though we had a good idea Dad would be coming.

Halloween time I could anticipate Mom and Dad spooning together on the sofa. We were out running around with our friends trick-or-treating, and we would come back in, catching them by surprise. Whatever the reason, I enjoyed the warm feeling this sparked inside me.

Hayrides and Halloween seemed to go together in this small Midwestern hideaway. We were not living in the country, but in a rather rural setting, being just a little removed from the big city life.

Hayrides were another opportunity to star gaze. That, in combination with the sweet smell of the straw, was home to me.

One night, around age nine, voices and flashing lights awakened me. Gina came running in the room and delightedly shrieked, "Come on, come see Judy. She's floating in the boat!"

Judy, our brown and white-spotted Labrador-mix dog, had always been part of the family. Being part hunting dog, she perpetually brought birds and rodents back to our home. She occupied a great deal of her time in these endeavors. Being cleanliness minded, I did not want to mix with the germ infestations, so declined to get too close to her. I loved her just the same.

It dawned on me that Gina had left her bed, even though the moonlight still shone through the window. Instead, she came running into our shared abode. "What?" I retorted, "What do you mean Judy's floating?"

"Come see!" she reiterated. Grabbing a blanket, I drowsily dragged myself down the hallway to check out the commotion. As I sauntered, I realized that there were flashing lights outside the front windows. Not only that, but they were coming from a fire truck parked right in our driveway! Mom and Dad were not in their bedroom, nor David. Only David's snakes and lizards were visible in their respective cages, as I made my way past to join the clamor, now clearly taking place in the kitchen. Seeing the family huddled around the utility room door near the kitchen, which led to the basement below, was a funny sight. They were excitedly talking and laughing at such a pace, it was difficult to make out what had taken place.

Soon it was evident that the basement had flooded. Judy had climbed into my dad's fishing boat, carried her puppies in with her, and they were now floating on the floodwater in the basement below. There was also talk of a danger. I heard something about the water reaching the pilot light on the furnace. We had to get out of the house.

The next thing I knew we were on our way to Grandma's house. That was OK by me. I loved going to Grandma's. Everyone behaved at their best and besides that, she always had some kind of treat. I knew I felt loved and accepted. When I entered high school, Grandma made a quilt for me with lots of fabric scraps that were remnants of sewing projects. I still have it. It's soft and gentle, like her.

That year I turned eleven. It marked a turning point in my life.

Gina and I were watching television. She wanted me to change the channel. I said, "No, I want to watch this show." She was not happy. She proceeded to leap around the room, trying to block my view from seeing the show, until I became annoyed enough that I chased her. She sprang up on the sofa, feet first. I followed behind her. She jumped off. When I came down, my toes got stuck between the wooden frame and the cushions. I slammed face-first onto the vinyl floor below. As I leaned forward, I began manipulating my mouth to form a scream. No sound came out. The only thing visible was teeth, as my mouth widened to project a cry for help.

At least there used to be teeth. My two front teeth were broken. Not only broken, there was nothing there. Nothing. Zilch. The only thought running through my head as my tongue surmised the damage was, *Now I'm going to have false teeth*!

There would be a lot more damage done than broken teeth, but I didn't know it at the time.

CHAPTER 4

MOVING FORWARD

Wedding invitations lay stacked in rows against the wall under the tall bay windows. My roommate Belinda shared the small apartment. As a nurse who worked the night shift, she and I rarely crossed paths. The same Iowa town held the location of my job as a kindergarten teacher at a small private school. At age twenty-four, I felt time slipping away. My sister Gina, two years younger, had just married in March. I could feel a competitive sibling tug having sway in my decisions. *But really, how had I gotten to this place?* I sat staring at the invitations, and thought, *Do I mail them, or do I mail them not, do I mail them, or do I mail them not?* Doesn't everyone have doubts anticipating their upcoming wedding? I couldn't cancel my plans, as my parents had already spent a lot of money. I could feel a knot in my stomach that had been growing for some time, but my brain put up a good argument.

Everything had seemed like it was meant to be.

Mark and I were friends in college, so when he called over the Christmas holiday and asked to get together, it seemed natural. Only seconds before I had been cleaning through a drawer and ran across old letters from him, and pondered, *I wonder what he is doing? He's probably married by now.* The words of a song came back to me with such force, that I stopped my paper shuffling, and sang:

Trust in the Lord, wait patiently for him, and he shall give thee
Thy heart's desire, Oh trust in the Lord, wait patiently for him,
and he shall give thee thy heart's desire.
-author unknown

It had been years since I'd thought of those words. And even then, I had only been introduced to the song briefly. An image of playing the piano, while Mark sang standing next to me, pressed forward in my mind. He had asked for me to play while he rehearsed for the voice lessons he took. I did it as a favor, but had to hide my reactions as he sang completely and utterly, off-key. The ringing of the phone interrupted my thoughts.

"Carrie?" a male voice uttered.

"Yes, who is this?" I queried.

"This is Mark. I'm in town for Christmas break. I wondered if you might want to get together," he stated hopefully.

My mouth fell open, while my brain jittered. Following numerous frozen seconds, I tumbled forth with, "What did you have in mind?"

"I could cook for you, say, chicken and rice, salad, and Baked Alaska?" he carefully relayed.

Baked Alaska, is he kidding? I didn't even know how to make that! "When?" I spat out.

I fleetingly remembered that I had an invitation to a party for the next evening with another male friend, Ben, who was an artist for American Greeting Cards. I had spent some time with him, and found him intriguing.

While lost in thought, I barely heard his reply, "Tomorrow night." Ugh, I didn't want to hurt my friend Ben, but it sounded like Mark had plans to be in town only a short time. Ben and I had only gone out a few times, but he'd bought me a Christmas present and I could tell he had developed a fondness for me, maybe even hoping for more.

So I told him, "OK, what do you want me to get for you?"

"I'll bring everything I need, if you just have the staples like flour and salt," he gushed.

"OK, what time?" I inquired.

"Is 4:00 alright, so I have time to cook and then we are not eating too late?" he asked.

"That sounds good. See you then." I hung up. *What had I just done?* Destroyed a close friendship with Ben, for a possible "rendezvous" with Mark, whom I had never found attractive?

What was I thinking? It must be the flattery. He always acted as if I was perfect. What girl wouldn't like that? I guess my more curious side wanted to see how he'd changed since it had been a few years after our encounters at college. *Maybe he'd matured, now that time had passed.*

I recalled how, in English Literature class, he'd "dropped his pants," during an assigned presentation. He had on swim trunks underneath, but I never forgot the horror and embarrassment I felt while witnessing the outlandish event.

The part I couldn't shake was how he'd called right when I thought of him, and the haunting words of the song that had flooded my being.

The evening felt a little awkward starting from the moment I opened my door. Mark sported a curly afro, which was radically different from the short, conservative cut he had worn in college. A serenity surrounded him that I did not recognize. He moved about in the kitchen as if he were accustomed to cooking regularly, and with ease. I watched carefully while he made Baked Alaska, and marveled at the outcome.

Needless to say, he impressed me. At some point, he asked to play my guitar, and began playing and singing with a mellow voice I did not know. He humored me with how he'd spent many snowy, cold, and lonely nights in Wisconsin where he taught, learning to play and sing.

As I observed how he'd developed himself in so many ways, some flutters of attraction were sparked within me.

While sitting on the sofa and watching him clean up, a mysterious air twisting and turning between us, wrapped around me, and grabbed my attention in a way that would not let go. This experience, along with his persistence and interest in me, drew me to respond to the many letters and phone calls that would follow.

In February, I had plans to go skiing with a group of young adults, including a close friend, Cheryl. We were taking a bus to Michigan. Cheryl and I had worked together at Macy's for several summers in-between semesters, in my hometown in Iowa. She had not gone to college, but rather, worked full-time for the company. She did quite well, became a manager, and enjoyed many employee benefits. When I graduated, I continued working for Macy's, but left in September, to teach at a private school. My friendship with Cheryl lingered and we were looking forward to spending this quality time together.

As the time neared, I mentioned to Mark that I would be skiing in Michigan over the holiday weekend in February. He immediately began asking questions about the exact days and times, and where we would be staying. An uneasiness rested with me during these conversations. *How would I tell him that I didn't want him to go?* I began feeling my freedom slip away, but it seemed I had no choice but to have him meet us there. He reasoned that the closeness to Wisconsin made it the perfect opportunity for us to get together. I relinquished.

It seemed that no matter what Cheryl and I did, or where we went during that trip, he stayed close by, like a puppy panting behind. When I made an observation to that effect, we ended up in an argument. He said I should have told him if I didn't want him to go. I said he didn't give me much choice, with his persistence. That trip served to put a snowdrift between us.

It wasn't long after our return home, however, that the phone calls and letters continued.

His flowery compliments made it easy to forget the conflicts we had endured during the trip.

He regularly sent poems that contained that same mystical air which had allured me while he wore an apron in my kitchen. He convinced me to visit him in Wisconsin, during the spring break.

The fresh air and rolling hills of northern Wisconsin had a feel of home. The open spaces were refreshing, after having spent so much time close to a big city. We drove through the immense lands, heading to nowhere in particular. We listened to the sounds of John Denver through the eight track player in his dash. We talked of our hopes and dreams. It was 1979.

Only a month earlier, I'd been running on the high school track with my roommate at the time, Christy (another nurse, surprise).

Looking up at the star sprinkled sky, I had an overwhelming sense that something important would soon be taking place in my life. I felt an excitement as this notion crept into the corners of my mind.

As we traveled the hilly terrain of Cheesehead territory, Mark told me of a dream in which he'd been told to ask me to marry him. He then said, "Did I want to marry him?"

I said, "I can't think of any reason why not to marry." He continued with, "I can move to Iowa. We could get married this summer." My spirit stirred, crowding out the quiet voices of reason. Yes, maybe getting married would be the big event I had perceived. Since we were both teachers, we would have our summers and holidays together. I would be able to marry the same year as my sister, and not wait any longer. Time seemed to rush forward as the pace quickened with thoughts of moving and wedding plans filled my mind.

Soon after he moved, we went to a movie. A movie so hilariously funny, that I nearly rolled in the aisle, laughing. I remember looking over at Mark, and seeing only a stalwart expression on his face, not even the crack of a smile. Wow, how could he not laugh at a Chevy Chase movie? Surely he must not be feeling well, and this was unusual. *I couldn't think about that, we were getting married.*

The decision had been made.

The letter arrived in my mailbox that I had long awaited. The acceptance letter into graduate school. I could attend Iowa State University and receive my masters in Social Work. I didn't really want to be a social worker, but rather, could use the degree to be a counselor. I wanted to help others, as I'd been helped through high school when I sank into a depression that had been difficult to shake. It just so happened that the university was located in Ames, Iowa, the same town where Rick lived. I felt compelled to call Rick.

"Rick?" I questioned, after dialing.

A long silence followed, and then, "Yes?" on the other line.

"This is Carrie," I carefully ventured.

"Uh-huh, what's up?"

"I wanted to tell you that I got accepted into Iowa State's MSW program," I chirped.

"That's great," he stated cautiously.

"What else is up?" he reiterated, like a mouse poking at a piece of cheese, caught in a trap.

"I'm getting married this summer," I tossed back, while the mousetrap slammed shut.

"Who's the lucky guy?" he uttered.

"Mark Cunningham, from college," I offered.

"You deserve each other," he darted back. "Well, that's OK, because I have a friend who cooks for me and we are getting along very well."

Why did I feel pain when we were no longer together? Why had I really called him? What just happened during the phone call? Confusion encircled me.

I was anxious to share the news with Mark. His response dampened my enthusiasm, however, as he said, "If you are going to graduate school, we are not getting married." *What?* I halted in my mental tracks as thoughts whirled past *Why not? What is he saying?* Through our conversations, he poured syrup over the questions, until they no longer stuck. I slowly opened my clutched hand, and let the future I had planned, sift through my fingers. I would have to go to graduate school some other time.

As the wedding approached, we went miniature golfing with my sister Gina, and new brother-in-law, Keith. I thought we were having fun, but Mark didn't do so well. The tension mounted, as we rounded each corner to a new contest. Each time Mark's ball missed a hole, and his score grew, he muttered under his breath with frustration. Without warning, we heard a blood-curdling yell as he flung the golf club across the park. A stunned silence followed. I felt the need to "cover-up" the moment, with chatter and laughs to mend the crack in our time together. No apologies were issued, with no discussion about what had occurred. There was however, a look of trepidation from Gina directed to me, as if to say, "What are you doing?" I don't think she was thinking only of the golf game.

Well, that's only one incident, it'll never happen again, I thought.

I was wrong.

I was so very wrong.

CHAPTER 5

MY STORY BEGINS

We were near our destination. Billows of fog greeted us as we rounded each curve of the narrow cliffside highway, until we were enveloped in marshmallow crème. We'd seen many interesting landscapes as we drove cross-country, but nothing could compare to the rapture that quickly surrounded us. Darkness closed in, while glimpses of the seashore were still visible in-between the white patches, each time taking my breath in waves of "oh's" and "oooh's." The splendor of the cypress trees bowed in the foreground. The combination of all these elements painted the perfect backdrop for romance. Perhaps this would make up for the tediously long, hot and sticky trip we'd just endured in our Mazda sports car.

How had he talked me into spending all of my two thousand dollar savings account for the deposit on a new car, one that didn't even have air conditioning? "It's no longer important," he'd said. I had worked hard to save money for grad school, but I didn't resist. He won, and a piece of me died, along with my dream. Those things were all behind us now, because we were in Monterey, California for our honeymoon.

It was July 1979.

The memory of The Pirates of the Caribbean ship ride was still fresh in my mind. We had just left Disneyland the day before. Mark refused to go on any roller coaster rides, so I spent most of the day going on rides by myself. When we went on the ship ride, he joined in, but yelled out when we approached running water. I was embarrassed. I didn't know why he wanted to go to Disneyland if he didn't like going on rides. After a short one day stay, we were driving north to Monterey Inn.

We pulled into the inn late, after our descent from the steep drive. Our stay would prove to be the highlight of the many days and months that were ahead of us. The first day after our arrival, we spent in bed, part exhaustion, and part curiosity, to explore the possibilities of our new existence. The bellhop peered into the room to satisfy his own curious nature, while making meal deliveries. We were like children, finally getting to taste the candy on the forbidden shelf, both having been virgins. The rest of our time was spent barefoot on the soft, white-sanded beaches, with wind blowing through our hair. We were free of responsibilities, at least for a while.

Too soon, it came time to leave this land of wonderment. As we made the ascent from Monterey, we would also experience the sharp contrast between this fantasyland and our reality.

Our next stop was in a suburb of Salt Lake City, Utah for a wedding reception with Mark's family and friends. We had married in a large church in Iowa, with a crowd that nearly filled the lower level. The words from our wedding came back to me now, as I remembered:

> *Guided by some unseen hand, our paths came together, from the distances of time and space . . . .*

Many of his family and friends had been unable to attend the wedding. The Utah reception had been held in a church, in a reception hall, with dinner served. The room filled wall to wall with aunts, uncles, cousins, and his sister, brother-in-law, and parents, along with a sprinkling of other attendees, mostly church friends. The reception served as my first acquaintance with most of them.

After several more days of driving, we returned to Iowa with only a few days to settle in and get ready to teach. I would be teaching 5th grade, as would he. It was quite a leap from the class of twelve kindergartners I'd had the year before. Although the class had only eighteen students, I found myself being stretched out of my non-assertive self into a very uncomfortable space. Several of the students would challenge me with questions that I could not answer. I didn't know at the time that it would have been better to not make that revelation, but rather, respond with questions such as "I wonder who could look up that answer for us?" I lacked the experience in life, and in teaching, that would have armored me with the insight or skills I needed. That made for a very difficult year, in all ways.

It was early morning, and we were getting ready for work. I made breakfast and left it on the counter for Mark. He shoved the plate at me and said angrily, "I don't eat breakfast!" I remember feeling devastated, because in my mind, that's what a good wife did, made breakfast for her husband.

I kept thinking, surely he's just having a bad morning, so I kept trying. I tried different kinds of breakfasts. I thought maybe I didn't fix the right kind of food. I got the same response. So I finally quit trying. *Did I do something wrong?* The knot in my stomach came back. *I would have to work harder to please him*, I thought. That's what a wife is supposed to do.

In the bedroom, I also tried to be "the good wife." I remember one night, early on, when I felt a wave of energy or spirit that passed over me when we made love. When I commented on it, he screamed, "There you go bringing religion into the bedroom!! What's wrong with you?!"

He went on and on, as he stormed out of the room. I just thought, *Gosh, what WAS wrong with me?*

The pain hurled me back to our wedding night, when, after making love for the first time, he'd said, "Is that all there is to you?" As a clueless virgin, I didn't know for sure if he referred to my small-framed figure, or his experience of me, sexually. I trembled to ask. I didn't know if he even knew the answer. I did know one thing for sure. I saw and felt his unhappiness. He oozed of unhappiness. I sought to make him happy.

So, we had sex, without foreplay, without tenderness, and without excitement. I came to accept that there would be no "love making." At least, it didn't feel like love. I guessed that I wasn't supposed to enjoy it. I disconnected myself from the spirit I had felt, and came to accept compliance as my way of life. I made frequent visits to the doctor's office for very painful chronic cystitis, that frequently would go straight to bleeding. I had one infection after another, until I found a book to prevent them. The doctors didn't help. They just kept giving me more medicine. They didn't know I needed a lot more than any medicine could give me.

It seemed that no matter what I did, it wasn't the right thing. I couldn't fix anything, no matter how hard I tried. As the darts were hurled, I started curling up inside. The more pain I felt, the more confused I became. *Didn't he marry me because he loved me? Why didn't any of this feel like love?* These thoughts chased me everywhere I went, with no way of escaping.

Whatever fleeting joy I experienced, and whatever fantasies I'd had in my mind, quickly dissolved in those early days. Memories as thick as molasses poured over me as I remembered the love I had experienced with Rick. The sweetness dissipated quickly with, *I can't think about him, I'm married.* The stark reality of the choice I had made sank me into a grief that would haunt even my brightest days. I grieved lost love, I grieved the loss of joyful fantasies, and I grieved my future. Not only that, but I felt very alone. I wouldn't tell anyone. I felt like such an utter and complete failure.

Looking around the living room in our small apartment, my head filled with whirling thoughts, like tornadoes, barely touching ground long enough for me to grasp them. *You made your bed, now lie in it,* was an adage spoken with conviction by my father. I thought that must surely apply to me now. *I must have made a terrible mistake, and I can't even get an annulment because my marriage had already been consummated.* My parents paid lots of money for my wedding. How could I get out from under that expense? What about the embarrassment they would feel, and that I would feel? It would be so humiliating! As I stood looking around our living room, memories of my mother singing, "To Dream the Impossible Dream," rode past, and along with it, the determination that I would make my marriage work no matter what. With that one decision, my fate for the next seventeen years was rolled out in front of me.

The words of the song came back to me.

To dream, the impossible dream . . .

CHAPTER 6

FINDING A HOME

We were driving through neighborhoods looking at houses. It was spring and, you might say, "everything was coming up roses." At least the air was hopeful. Just a few weeks earlier Mark had said, "Let's buy a house."

I queried, "With what money?"

We could buy a house without much money," he responded, "I owned my house in Wisconsin."

I liked the idea of living near my family, but not too close, so we still had our own lives.

We were in Fort Dodge, Iowa, and my family was in Des Moines, Iowa, about an hour's drive away. My sister Gina lived there, as well as my parents, and other extended family. My brother David lived an hour farther west and south of Des Moines, so I saw him less frequently.

He was two years older than me. We had not been as close growing up, as Gina and I, but being the middle child meant we were closest in age. We'd always had lots of family get-togethers through the years, not only for the bigger holidays, but to celebrate birthdays and other occasions as well. I liked being part of those events. If we bought a house, that would give some permanency to our living situation. I felt some glimmers of excitement.

When we discovered that we could, indeed, buy a house, the reality planted itself even more firmly in my mind. Let's see, we would need more furniture, and we would need a washer and dryer. My head spun with the new ventures that were in sight. We looked at three bedroom, two bath houses, that had two car garages and downstairs recreation rooms. I grew up in a three bedroom, two bath house, so it fit my idea of middle class America, and it had begun to be in my reach, far sooner than I would have imagined.

We settled on a house that fit our needs perfectly. It would have everything we needed already in place, including the refrigerator, and washer and dryer. Here we were, married only a year, and moving into our first house. Life began to brighten for me. Maybe shifts were occurring for the better.

Our energies turned to setting up our new home. We moved, decorated, and planned with all our spare time. I began feeling like a wife and homemaker. This is what I'd always dreamed about. *This is the way it should be.* Like our sports car, we went speeding full-steam ahead getting settled into our new home. Days and weeks were consumed with our doting attention on every detail of our house, as we strove for perfection.

When we had everything in place, we decided to do some entertaining. We invited friends over who happened to have a two-year old daughter. Dinner ended up rushed, as the two-year old, Sasha, didn't want to sit for long. I enjoyed experiencing a little one around the house. She was so cute that I found myself fantasizing about what it would be like to have my own child.

After dinner, we wandered into the living room to visit while we let our dinners settle. I felt some relief, having the pressure off me, as the cook. I didn't mind cooking, but I did not consider myself a great cook, and I definitely didn't like being the center of attention as the menu items were being scrutinized. Mark however, didn't hesitate to praise me as being the best.

Sometimes he surprised me with his complimentary gushes, at least in public, like a trophy to be shined and placed on the shelf for everyone to see and comment on. It made me uneasy, but I grabbed at everything I could get. *Maybe he did love me after all.*

"DON'T TOUCH THAT," interrupted my thoughts as I jerked my head in the direction of the window where Sasha caressed the drapes. Mark's voice boomed across the room the second he saw what she was doing. My mouth gaped open while I tried to think what I could say or do to cover up the tension of the moment. Why couldn't she touch the drapes? Surely she wouldn't hurt them. I was bewildered. I saw the pained and shocked looks on the faces of Sasha's parents.

I smiled and made a remark about her cuteness, but I sensed that it didn't erase the truth of what had just happened.

Looking at the intense emotion on Mark's face did not give any clues about his reaction.

I had gotten pretty good at reading his moods, but this one did not reveal itself. I didn't know how to interpret it. As a teacher, it couldn't be that he didn't like kids, but his anger was much stronger than the situation would seem to elicit. The evening ended shortly after the curtain incident, and I don't remember them ever coming to our house again. I couldn't blame them. Just when I thought we were getting somewhere, this only added to my growing loneliness and uncertainties.

Summer soon flowed into fall. Mark sat on the edge of the bed, gasping for his every breath, and it was the middle of the night. We didn't know it at the time, but he was developing asthma.

He hurled his words freely, as he strained to take air in, and release it, with belabored breaths.

"I hate it here. I can't stand it. I can't even breathe. I'm surrounded by a bunch of Midwest hicks. I'm miserable!!" he gushed.

Arrows hurled straight at my heart. *Midwestern hicks? Was he talking about me and my family? He hates it here? Does that mean we have to move? We had only just bought our house!*

Why is he having trouble breathing? Fear for his ability to breathe served as a wall that kept me from getting the answers to questions that hung on a suspension bridge in mid-air. An icy silence filled the space between us, except for his breathing. A heaviness filled my own chest as

I listened to the words being spewed out, amidst the heaves and sighs of his emotional turmoil.

Too much to take in and it's too difficult to understand, I thought. I would think about it some other time. *I'm too tired to think now*, and so I drifted off, hoping that it would all just go away so I could go back into the fantasies of my inner world.

The settling in of winter quieted Mark's pleas for being elsewhere, with the shift in the weather. I thankfully held onto the solitude that had settled in along with it. Yet, more of a distance had been growing between us. At night, it seemed more and more that he stayed up later, while I drifted into slumber. One night I wandered downstairs to find him adjusting the television antennae. I asked him what he was doing, to which he grew angry.

"What do you mean, what am I doing? I'm adjusting the antennae to get channels on the television!"

"What kind of channels are you trying to get?" I asked.

"I have it hooked up to get cable, and I'm trying to get more channels," he stated matter of factly.

"You act like what you're doing is a secret," I observed.

"No, it doesn't matter anyway," he firmly responded. "Go back to bed, it's late," he added curtly.

I left the room, feeling dazed and with a bad taste in my mouth. I didn't like the idea that he was behaving suspiciously, and keeping something secretive as well. I was perplexed because Mark went to church and was a minister. *Why would he do something he felt he needed to hide?? What did he watch that was so important to him?* I couldn't let go of those thoughts, so I began getting up at night to peer into the basement to get glimpses of the television. I soon had at least part of the answers I sought. I could see that he had been watching the Playboy channel. *Wasn't I enough? Did he choose these shows over me?* A sickening feeling began to churn within.

After that, I tried not to notice what happened at night. I felt overwhelmed and in pain.

He enjoyed trips downstairs as much or more as being in bed next to me. We continued at least a partial sexual relationship, when he felt like it. I noticed, however, that there were more and more comments about the ways he wanted me to change.

"Why don't you wear tall high heels? I don't like the shoes you wear. Why don't you wear red nail polish? You're not a woman unless you wear nail polish. Why don't you get breast implants? You're so small." I could not compete with the observations he made of his fantasy women. The pace with which the comments were pitched seemed to pick up, while I shrank smaller and smaller inside.

Thank goodness I had my career to fling myself into. He didn't like it, and would make observations about the amount of work I brought home, or how much time went into my teaching. He made a rule for himself to never bring work home. I tried, but it didn't work as well. I had decided to pursue a degree in school counseling, as a close second to social work. It gave me a sense of satisfaction that I would eventually still be doing what I really wanted. He started a degree as well, in school administration. We were both attending school in the summers.

The waves of despair began swelling upward and threatening to crash over me when he came home in the spring announcing, "I have to get the hell out of here and move back to Utah." As the words washed over me, I felt like I was drowning as I sputtered and choked with the reality of what he said. *What about my house? What about my family? What about the degree I'd started in school counseling?* The sand slipped from under my feet, and I could feel myself being washed far out to sea, losing my footing and sight of the shore of what had been life as I'd known it. I watched the sand castle of our home, being dissolved in the waves.

We were going to Utah.

CHAPTER 7

BLOOD, SWEAT AND FEARS

The San Joaquin Valley is known for its beautiful sunsets. As I gazed into the red, orange, and yellow hues of the horizon, I knew why. This was the view every night, from our ranch style brick house in the rural town of Merced, California. We had moved several times before owning a home again. I was glad to be in this place, with lots of land around us, including a large yard in back.

It was 1982.

We were once again settled, but it had definitely not been easy getting here.

When we left Iowa, we bought an old pick-up truck to hold our things. The truck, along with our cars, held all that we owned. We didn't have jobs when we left, and we were pretty stressed not knowing where we would end up. Adding to the stress were situations we encountered traveling west.

At one point, we stopped at a truck stop to eat lunch. Mark gazed across the room at some bikers who looked like they'd walked straight out of Hell's Angels, chains and all. One of them screamed in Mark's direction and spewed, "What are you staring at?" Mark mumbled something like, "I am admiring your beard." Needless to say, we high-tailed it out of there, as the biker dude flipped us off!

Another time we were staying at a motel in Wyoming and there was a fly on the window.

Mark took hold of the curtain and swung it at the fly, breaking the window. He didn't know the curtain had a weighted corner. We hadn't counted on paying for the expense of a broken window!

Our first stop was to live with Mark's parents for a few weeks, in Salt Lake City, Utah, but when we realized there were no job opportunities, we knew we needed to move on. Mark had hoped we would be able to live near his parents in their beautiful mountain town. We ended up heading for California, and stayed in a mobile home for another month or so, while we pursued jobs in the Sacramento area.

Again, no jobs appeared.

We were beginning to consider that we were going to have to go back to school in order to be able to teach in California. Consequently, we had to get jobs under "emergency credentials," which made a difficult hiring situation. Finally, in the southern valley town of Chowchilla, California, we secured positions a few days before school started. Mark taught fourth grade, and I taught kindergarten. The town had a nickname as "The Little Mexico," because of the large Hispanic population.

We found a condo in the nearby town of Madera, California. It was a pretty setting, and I liked the newness of the décor. It became the setting of my first experience with an earthquake.

At about 3 a.m. I awakened to what I thought was someone jumping on the roof. The water in our bed "rocked and rolled." I yelled out, and Mark said, "Go back to sleep, it's only an earthquake." *A what?*! This house is also where I ran into the side of the garage, trying to back out. "What an idiot," Mark had jeered.

This valley was a foreign land of grape fields and dusty, dry air. Much of the year displayed a brown landscape, except for the leaves of the vines, and the orange and almond orchards, woven in-between. I grew to love the warm temperatures. I did not miss the snow and ice of the Midwest. However, I did grieve the loss of my family and friends, who were so far away. I negotiated with Mark to travel back home at least once every year or so. It softened the loneliness that had become my constant companion. We joined a church group that adopted us as family, which also eased the transition.

Teaching in Chowchilla was an entirely new experience for me. Between ninety and ninety-five percent of the students in my classroom did not speak English. I did not speak Spanish. I quickly developed sign language for "be quiet and sit down," and other key phrases that helped me to survive these babies, and assist in their learning. I also learned some brief commands in Spanish. They really were babies, which describes many kindergartners that are not quite ready for the rigor of the classroom environment.

I will always remember Miguel. He stood out, with his distinguished, light, wavy hair. I soon found out his uniqueness in other ways as well. One day we were using clay, and in the short time that I had my back turned, he had it smeared up and down his arms and all over his face. I think he put it in his mouth too. Another day, we were walking in line to the cafeteria, with its rather spectacular whole side of the building lined with windows. Miguel walked over to the landscaping in front of the windows and started peeing. Aw-chee-wah-wah, but he was so cute!

The one thing that stood out in working with these students was how little they had materially, and how deeply appreciative they were for every small thing in their world. For example, I loved to bring popcorn and share it with them because they would be delighted watching it pop, and enjoyed eating something that, for them, was a luxury.

My teaching experience became tainted, working at the same school with Mark. He ignored me while at school, acting like we were total strangers. Yet, he would flirt with many of the female teachers, in front of me. I didn't understand this kind of behavior, and when I questioned him about it, he would say, "We see each other all the time, why do we need to talk at school too?"

I remember one time in particular being especially painful. We had a school dinner function right before the holiday. We went to a fancy steakhouse where a band played near a large dance floor. After eating, some of the teachers went to dance and enjoy the music. Mark got up from the dinner table and went over to Sharon to ask her to dance. She glanced at me, briefly, and slurred in my direction, "You don't mind do you?" She didn't wait for my response, before she whisked off with him into the other room. Everything happened so quickly that I scarcely had time to absorb it, let alone respond. I felt myself slightly nodding, "no," as I felt everyone looking my way to see what I would do.

Memories of myself as a little ten year old who'd just gotten rejected by her best friend came flooding back to me. Karen, my next-door neighbor, enjoyed "downsizing" me when we were at school. I think a lot of it came from the fact that I made good grades and she didn't. Also, teachers tended to befriend me, because I made a "good, quiet, cooperative," student, ripe material for a "teacher's pet."

We were on the playground and she walked over to me, then said, "I won't be sitting next to you on the bus for the fieldtrip, I'm sitting next to Debbie." I felt my world cave in, and the tears started to flow. I remember other girls pointing and laughing and making fun of me.

Those same tears were creeping over the dam now, as the reality of what had just happened, sank in. Sharon, an especially flirtatious teacher, wore everything bra-less. *How did she get away with it?* It seemed it could only happen in this God-forsaken town of Chowchilla, California.

Mark loved it. He thought she epitomized wonderful, because she allowed him full viewing of her bouncy cleavage. I resented her. She only seemed to exacerbate what I lacked, not only her cleavage, but her carefree spirit. My own spirit became more and more depressed, and unavailable. I resembled a wounded animal, not knowing what to do except lick my wounds.

Lick my wounds, and live my new mantra, "Be tough." That kicked in now, as I fought with everything in me to not run out the door and drive away. *I would show him, I'll take the car, and he'll be left without transportation.* Wow, that would just drive him into getting into a car with Sharon. Is it really what I wanted? So instead, I sat and pretended I was somewhere else, while outwardly trying to fight back the tears and continue acting friendly.

I was, after all, at a party.

On the way home, and afterwards, we had a big fight.

I fired my anger at him. He railed back with how I wasn't any fun. He also let me know that I had refused to dance with him in the past. I reminded him that it was because he jerked around in provocative ways, in public. Did it matter how I felt? There was no resolution. He seemed smug that he had caused a reaction in me. I felt, once again, that somehow something was wrong with me. *Did I make too much of the situation?* I felt confused. His flowery words smoothed over the conflict and made it less pervasive. "Wow, I'm married to the popular Carrie Turner. She never gets mad, but look at her now! You're turning me on," he teased. There could be no solution when he kept dodging my feelings.

Soon after beginning to teach, I continued taking classes, since I needed to acquire my teaching credential for the state of California. It was easy enough to get my master's degree at the same time. I attended Cal State Fresno in the summers, as well as during the school year.

An hour's commute each way made it a huge commitment of time and energy.

The counseling program was intense. We were critiqued behind a two-way mirror. If we did not pass, we had to re-take the complete course. This happened to many of my peers. Thankfully, it did not happen to me. The program did serve as a diversion from the tension I felt at home. It also gave me the satisfaction of knowing that I was taking care of myself, at least in my career. It helped me to fill the lonely hours, and it helped me to connect with other women and develop some friendships in the area.

What I didn't expect was to get more in touch with myself, in the process. One of the classes we had to take was "Group Counseling." In that class, we had to be in a group and share our issues. It scared me to share personally in front of everyone in class. I discovered that I had been grieving far more than I imagined. In addition to the moves and disappointments in my marriage, a close girlfriend from childhood summer camps, had died in a car accident. The grief poured out of me whenever I shared.

I did not, however, share anything related to my marriage.

I felt a need to protect Mark, to protect our marriage, and to protect our image as a couple.

Part of this need stemmed from our involvement in the church.

One night I returned home from school to find Mark very upset. He had just found out that his parents were divorcing. His grief and anger poured from him as he said, "They are supposed to be there for their grandkids! Why is this happening? Why is it happening to me?"

Pure exhaustion set in, as I watched the clock approach 10:00 at night. I had just returned from Fresno after a long day and lots of driving. As I readied myself for bed and lay down, his anger turned towards me. "Why was I always gone? I was supposed to be there for him. All I thought about was myself." *What?! I thought he supported me for going to school. What was happening?* It felt like he were treating me as if I had divorced him, not his parents divorcing each other.

It became too much. Sweat poured over me, and my heart began palpitating through my chest. I felt as if I couldn't breathe. I suffocated, and panted for every breath. *What was happening? Stop, stop the words from coming at me. Please, please stop.* The stop sign was up, but the car kept racing through, mowing me down in the process.

It was a panic attack. I think that's what it's called.

CHAPTER 8

MORE BLOOD, SWEAT AND FEARS

*J*ust keep putting one foot in front of the other, one day at a time, I told myself.

That's what enabled me to keep moving forward. I soon discovered that what I learned in my counseling program would help me in my personal life. I gained strength I didn't have before. Through the empowerment gained with knowledge and understanding, I began being able to separate myself, a little bit at a time, from Mark's reactions to me. That, in addition to the power of prayer, made me a survivor. God had become my best friend. I talked to him about everything.

One such occasion happened when Mark applied for school administration jobs. It seemed that no matter how many interviews, he just couldn't land a position. Eventually, he did secure a job as vice principal in a small town a ways east from where we lived. We decided to move further in, closer to his new job. This meant renting again, and also that I had to look for another job. I began teaching 2nd grade in a rural school in Pinedale, California, the same town where we had taken up residence. The school suited me well. 2nd grade was my favorite age to teach, and the teachers there were very down to earth. I found that I connected easily with them.

We found a house to rent, so that we weren't back in an apartment. I delighted in this, after having owned houses. Spaciously sprawled on a very wide street, they were beautiful homes with professional landscaping. I would be able to enjoy my living space, in spite of everything. I thought I would finally get to fulfill my dream of being an at-home mom. Since Mark made a lot more money, the hope existed that it could be a reality for me.

I was going to have a baby. Everything rode smoothly along as planned. I had wanted to get pregnant after completing my degree. Mark resisted. He had not yet started his new position when we found out the news. I pushed hard. After all, I turned thirty soon and my fertile days would be over. At least that's what I read. He let me know that he did not feel ready to have a child yet. I wondered if he would ever be ready. I felt he owed it to me, at the least, with the many roller coaster rides he'd taken me on. So, I persisted, and won.

At least I thought I'd won. The more pregnant I became, the nastier he became. As my body changed, he rejected me even more, and called me "fatso" and told me to get out of the car to open the garage door, and asked for my subservience in other ways. I remember when we went to visit his aunt. He decided we would stay in a church for the night, instead of staying in a motel, so we just slept on the floor. I felt humiliated to be in that situation, and suffer so miserably. *Didn't every man struggle with the idea of becoming a father, and giving up his freedom? Even so, did I deserve this treatment?*

Glancing into the mirror, I remember feeling very old. It was the first time I noticed wrinkles forming around my eyes. I said to myself, I wonder where that Mary Kay lady is, who wanted to sell to me a while back? In all seriousness, I did make a decision to buy in that fleeting mirror-moment. Unfortunately, I knew that neither Mary Kay, nor anyone else for that matter, would be able to save me from the body encounters of the contorted kind, that was my new reality. Only those who have been pregnant can understand.

That is why I consider Jan a true gift from God. She taught 3rd grade in the classroom next door to me. We experienced pregnancy at the same time. In fact, we ended up delivering within six weeks of each other. We compared notes all along the way, from our tired feet, to our sleepless nights. (Although my sleep wasn't TOO interrupted, since we had a warm waterbed.) I clung to the companionship I felt with her. We even had a joint baby shower which our co-workers and the Parent Teacher Association sponsored for us. I felt a little guilty because she had been a long time teacher at the school, while it was only my first year. They were very generous and welcoming, all the same.

One night as I took what I thought would be a relaxing shower, I saw Mark's hand reach in towards the spout. He shifted the temperature all the way around to the highest level in the hot range. In a split second I felt scalding water on my belly, as I lunged towards the faucet to get it turned off. I shrieked in agony, dying a thousand deaths, as I feared the worst. Maybe something terrible had happened to my baby. Never mind the redness to my skin, or the pain of the heat. I worried about what might be happening below the surface. Pain of this kind was indescribable.

He said he meant to turn on the cold. "I only kidded around," were his words.

At night, I found myself feeling very vulnerable lying next to Mark. He would make remarks that stung, and make it difficult for me to find peace. The mantra that he slung at me was, "Don't you dare have a boy. I don't think I could handle it." *What would I do? How could I choose whether we were to have a daughter or a son?*

I desperately prayed for a daughter. I didn't know what else I could do. I remember a lot of difficult moments when I would go out to lie on the couch. I would cry until I didn't have any tears left. I refused to allow myself to stay in bed at these moments, because then he would reject me for crying. At those times I would be in such gut-wrenching pain, that I could feel my baby churning and turning inside me.

The fall before our baby would be born, the onslaught of Mark's remarks intensified. In my stronger moments I realized that it wasn't about my image at all. It was more about him, that somehow as he tried to re-create me, that he fulfilled a need in himself to make him look or feel better. I learned that as I responded as he wanted, it didn't fix anything. Wearing nail polish didn't make anything right. It didn't really make him happier. It didn't make me happier. It didn't make things better between us.

The pain of not being loved, accepted, and cherished for who and what I was, became unbearable. I perceived myself as a mere image that he created, or maintained. Even though I had developed these understandings, somehow, it became even harder while I underwent one of the most vulnerable times of my life.

My vulnerability intensified with the onset of my weak emotional state as I entered the realm of the unknown land of childbirth and motherhood. My mind went back to the former spaces of, *I thought he loved me. I thought he really cared about me. Where did that person go? What was he doing to me? What was wrong? Was it really me? What was wrong with me? Please make it go away, it hurts so much. I don't even know who I can talk to.* God is my only friend. He is the only one that really understands and sees everything that I'm going through. So God is the one I cry out to. Many times, I couldn't form the words, only a mere cry came from the depths of my being, uttered in my sleep.

Our baby's due date was mid November, but I continued working until the 1st week of December, when I started having contractions, while teaching. I left, and drove myself to the hospital. Mark arrived within a few hours. The doctor said I had not progressed, and he wanted to run stress and non-stress tests, a sonogram, and all kinds of other exams to see what might be going on. The extensive tests revealed nothing, but he chose to further induce labor because I'd already been long over-due.

After sixteen hours of strong contractions, the doctor ordered an emergency C-section because the monitor showed the baby to be in distress. I chose to be knocked out because I didn't think I could bear the pain of disappointment on Mark's face, should we have a boy. The anesthesiologist held my hand as I went into a deep slumber.

He didn't know how much I needed that comfort. *He must be an angel,* I decided.

The doctor bet me an ice cream cone that the baby would be a boy. He said the sonogram pictures clearly showed that. I argued and said, "I think the baby is a girl."

"Carrie?"

"Yeah?"

"You have a baby girl," the nurse said into my ear, after rousing me.

I felt the faint turn of a smile on my drowsy face. The doctor would have to pay up on his bet. When I more fully awakened, the anesthesiologist came in to see me. He told me that with the cord wrapped around her neck several times, it could have been the reason I did not progress in labor. He said it had been a blessing, however, because if I had progressed on my own, the umbilical cord would have probably torn loose from the high position where it had been located, and would have caused life-threatening distress for both me and the baby. I thanked him for his part, and felt really blessed.

Thank you, God.

Mark came in and out of the room during my labor, more out of the room, than in. I think he spent most of his time in the bathroom. It wasn't much help to me, however. When I arrived back in my hospital room, he seemed happy that he had a daughter. Some of the tension that he had shown previously seemed to have relaxed now that the delivery was over, and he had a healthy girl.

Maybe now life would be a little smoother.

The hospital stay lasted for a whole week, as I acquired an infection. Mark came by for fleeting moments. My mother had spent time with me in November, when she thought the baby would be born, but had to go back when I didn't go into labor. Now, alone in the hospital, the reality of going through these new ventures on my own began to settle into my thoughts. Even the weather shifted, as the view out my window showed rain, rain, and more rain.

When we arrived back home, recovery from surgery progressed very slowly. I kept plugging along, getting up at night to feed her, and doing the routines throughout the day that she needed.

I found myself loving her even more each day. At night, when I nursed her in the rocking chair, I was aware of someone standing behind me, near my shoulder. When I turned and looked, I saw no one, yet I felt a tingling sensation that testified of another worldly being in my midst.

During the daytime, I felt that same presence moving around the corner as I walked down the hallway. It scared me. All I could think of was the angel of death. I thought perhaps the entity wanted to take her back into heaven. I began to pray earnestly about this strange presence that I sensed.

One night I awakened to what could best be described as a spiritual lullaby that I heard internally. I then understood in that moment that the angel, or presence, was there to comfort my child and ease her transition into this world. I prayed that I would not have the awareness any longer, because it scared me too much.

Soon after Erin, our daughter, was born, Mark came home from work expressing emotional distress about his work environment. He said his boss, the principal, would ask him to do something, and then come in and yell at him because he hadn't done it right, even though he felt he had followed directions that were being asked of him.

"No matter what I do, I'm not doing the right thing, he relayed." He kept saying, "I can't make it, I can't do this." The cloud of doom began settling over me when he talked like this.

One day, in January, he walked in and told me he'd quit.

I seethed in anger and hurt. I felt total devastation.

We had a baby! *Now I would no longer have a choice. I would have to go back to work.*

Where would he get a job now? What about my dream of him providing support for our family? How would I be able to work with a newborn baby? Who would take care of Erin? The walls crumbled around me with a loud roar of thunder.

There went my future, my dream, smoldering into an enormous cloud of dust . . .

CHAPTER 9

THE UPHILL CLIMB

"You bitch, now I can't divorce you. You went and had a baby."

Mark's words hurled past me, as he threw Erin's baby carrier down the hall. *Thank God Erin was not in it.* Mark's tantrums escalated as I became more preoccupied with Erin, and less available to him. His unhappiness multiplied as he took on substitute teaching positions, after having left his assistant principal position. The days were long while he meandered to find his way into a more permanent position. Finally, by spring he did acquire a full-time teaching position.

Just in time for me to return to work.

It was March 1986.

I struggled to find a sitter who would provide loving care for Erin. I found someone just before my first day back, but I felt unsettled. I didn't want to be working, and I resisted accepting my fate to return, while leaving Erin with a stranger.

When the school year ended, once again I returned home to spend the summer with Erin.

Mark felt secure in his new position so we could start talking about buying a home. We became captivated with the idea of having a new home built. We found what we were looking for in Madera, California, where we had lived in our first rental when we began teaching in Chowchilla.

I loved Madera, with its beautiful flowers and greenery. It was nestled off the freeway in it's own little hideaway. It felt far away from the dusty fields of Pinedale and Chowchilla. Sinus infections had become a way of life that I eagerly left behind. We got to pick out a floor plan, carpeting, where we wanted shelves, and lots of other exciting things that made me temporarily forget the pain that so frequently consumed me. I welcomed this intoxicating diversion.

In the meantime, Erin had become my constant companion. She became my buddy, and went everywhere with me. She changed me. A spirit resided in her from the day that she came into this world, that pierced me. I remember the first time she looked up at me and smiled with a sparkle in her eyes, as early as one day old. The vivacious spirit within her touched everyone who crossed her path. She wasn't afraid to talk to anyone, and easily engaged with total strangers. I, being very quiet and more into myself, was quickly drawn into talking to many different kinds of people in many different places, because of her.

The day finally arrived to move into our new home. We were becoming a family. Mark had fallen in love with Erin, and his behaviors seemed to shift more positively the less he saw her as an intrusion in his life, and more as a person. He seemed to treat me better, after having returned to my previously slender frame. He liked the newly obtained cleavage that pregnancy and nursing had blessed me with.

It was September 1986.

There was one incident, however, I remember where Mark stood on a ladder making some kind of repair when he got frustrated and flung the hammer. How many times would we be lucky enough to not be his target during his fits of anger? *I hoped and prayed it would never be the case. I kept thinking he would change.* I would get glimmers of hope. I wanted so much to fix him, but I couldn't. *The best I could do was to smooth over these situations when they occurred.*

That inhabited my way of thinking.

In February 1987, the doctor said, "I think we need to test Erin for Cystic's Fibrosis."

Cystic's Fibrosis? *What's that? It certainly didn't sound like a good thing.* Erin had been suffering extensively from allergic reactions to lots of different foods. Her legs had become spindly, and when she digested her food, it went through as foamy stools.

To cope, I found a book at the library about a girl who had the disease. I checked it out, thinking it would help me to understand more about what it meant. It turned out to be a heart-breaking story of a little girl who suffered a great deal with the illness and died an early death. I cried profusely while reading her story. I was strangled with horror. *Was that to be Erin's fate?*

Thankfully, the test turned out negative, but those were grueling weeks while we waited for the results.

While living in Madera, Mark purchased a motorcycle. It served as a toy for him, while struggling with the responsibilities of the grown-up world, or so it seemed to me. He spent time cruising in our little neighborhood now that we were settled down with Erin in our new house.

It was March 1987, when he came into the house and announced that his cousin Dan had passed out and fallen off his motorcycle.

"Maybe I should check with the doctor," Mark noted. "I am a carrier for the same kidney disease as my cousin, so maybe mine are not doing well either," Mark tossed out in a distressed tone. My heart skipped a beat, as I tried to digest what he said. *Didn't he get a clean bill of health when he went for a check-up before we were married?*

Now what?!

When Mark and I married, he'd said something about a kidney "condition" that ran in his family, but nothing ever came of it. A number of family members had the condition, but it didn't ultimately affect them. Nevertheless, I had insisted that he have a check-up before we got married.

I wanted to know what his health risks were, and thought he needed to be checked out.

Wasn't there something that needed to be done to prevent problems? Was there more to it? He had followed through with the check-up and told me that his kidney function had appeared fine, and there was nothing to worry about. That seemed contrary to what happened recently to his cousin.

It turned out that Dan had to go straight to dialysis. Mark panicked, and sold his motorcycle.

He said he didn't want to take a chance that he would be next. He went to the doctor's and found out his kidneys were also deteriorating. He also learned he had high blood pressure and started medication to lower it. Apparently high blood pressure can be deteriorative to the kidneys. He was informed that his kidney function would also eventually go, but that he could slow it down with the medication and a low protein diet.

Little did we know the road that lay ahead of us.

In a matter of a few short weeks, Mark decided that it would be best for us to move back to the Midwest because he now felt it was important to be near family. He considered my family to be closer to us, since his parents' divorce. My heart soared and grieved all at the same time. We would be leaving the house we had just built after only one short year. However, I would be able to pursue a school counseling position and use the degree I'd completed a few years earlier.

School counseling positions were plentiful in the Midwest. Erin and I would get to be near my family.

Once again we were selling a home, and loading a moving truck. It had become our way of life. Not one that I preferred. We ended up in a duplex in the same Iowa suburb where my sister Gina lived. Stress reigned, as we started all over again. Mark had been able to secure a teaching job, while I substituted until I found a more permanent position. It wasn't long before I saw the flirtatious Mark discover new conquests.

"Hi Melody, how's it going? You looked really hot in that yellow dress yesterday," Mark shared, while on the phone. "Yes, I know," Mark said softly. "Those heels you had on were really hot too," he continued. Mark had established female friendships in his new position, and he enjoyed having intimate phone conversations in front of me.

"What are you DOING?" screamed Mark, after hanging up the phone. "Can't I even have a phone conversation without you making noise?" he detailed.

"Why are you talking to women like that? You know, you're married. I don't like it when you talk to other women like that," I tentatively interjected.

"Oh, whatever," Mark slurred, ambushing my remarks like a fully loaded shotgun.

It appeared he thought I didn't deserve the same kind of conversations, and had no right to be disturbed by them.

I was numb.

I began to more fully lose touch with myself, as I desperately tried to separate from the pain I carried.

Within a short time, we were buying another new home. This time, we would be living in Des Moines, near my parents. We invested a great deal of energy into fixing up the house and yard. I loved gardening, and enjoyed planting a three-tiered flower garden in the front yard, leading up to the entryway. We completely re-did the backyard, tearing out overgrown bushes, and re-planting. This took our focus away from Mark's health and the other difficulties we continually encountered. His acceptance of me had not grown any greater, and he had the same difficulties adjusting to the Midwest that he'd had previously.

He still detested the weather.

He detested his strong allergic reactions.

He detested the Midwest mindset, which he attributed to me and my relatives.

As his challenges increased, so did his viewing of pornography. In spite of everything, we somehow managed to maintain a fairly regular sexual relationship. He would glorify whoever starred on the current video . . . what they looked like, and how they acted. I always came in second and less in some regard. He carried a mental list of his ideal woman, constantly compared it to me, and in his book, I always fell short. One time it would be Betsy Boobsy, and another time Bouncy Brunette, and another time someone else. His obsession felt nothing less than on-going affairs. It interfered with our being able to build a marriage together. It felt a lot less than loving, and I came out the loser.

One night, he kept "poking" at me, trying to get me to react.

He rarely saw me express anger.

"Wake up, Carrie," Mark mused, "Come on," he jabbed, "wake up, wake up, wake up," he continued to chide.

Go away, I'm exhausted, my mind recited.

Mark did not stop, he continued until I was seething with anger.

He had no regret for the anguish he caused me. In fact, he laughed. "I got you to get angry," he boasted. "Look at you, you're angry," he jeered.

Fully awake now, I knew I had to leave. *I had to get in the car and drive away. I didn't know where I would go, but I needed to get away.* I felt like a ticking time bomb.

I ended up in a parking lot, and just sat crying, until I had no more energy left.

Sometimes I just had to let it all out.

Within less than a year after moving into our new home, Mark became alarmed when he realized that the loss of his kidney function was eminent. The voice of reason kicked in when he said, "I think we should move back to California so that we have good health insurance. Here in the Midwest, teachers don't have as extensive health coverage as they do in California.

I no longer had any fight left in me.

I said I would go on one condition, that we could have a second child. "Erin needs a sibling, and I want a two child family," I reported, "I want another daughter."

"How can I agree to that when I don't even know if I'll be around to take care of them?" he said, "Besides that, how do you know it will be another girl?"

I told him that I understood it might mean I'd be taking care of a baby on my own. I also understood that there was no guarantee of a girl, but these were risks I would be willing to take.

He grimaced, but gave implied silent consent.

This time, he found a job in the San Francisco Bay area. We would not be returning to the valley. With the onset of his illness, Mark demonstrated a new air of humility that made it easier for me to connect with him. I felt compassion for him and his suffering, in spite of my own distress.

When he left to start his new job, Erin and I stayed behind to sell the house and prepare to move. I had been working as a school counselor and needed time to transition out of my position.

I spent my weekends marketing the house and showing it to interested parties. Success eluded me, so I decided the front of the house needed to be painted. Using an extension ladder, I painted, while Erin bounced back and forth playing in front yards within my view.

At night, I prayed. I prayed for our future. I prayed for Mark's health. And I prayed for him to find comfort in feeling my presence, as "my essence wrapped around him." That following night Mark called and said, "You'll never believe what happened to me last night."

I said, "What's that?"

He said, "I felt your spirit around me." I gasped. He proceeded to use the same words I had used in my prayer. I considered this to be another turning point in my life. At the time, I avidly read a book titled, *Power Evangelism*, by John Wimber. It had a profound effect on me, because up until then, I thought more in terms of us praying to God, and then God letting things happen or not happen, from him. I hadn't thought of our ability to make things happen for each other. As I read the book and absorbed the ideas presented, I experienced a tingling that surged through my hands, as a precursor to what I would later learn to be energy.

The idea that a person can actually send spirit to be with someone else was new to me.

Perhaps this kind of sharing by sending presence to someone close could only be possible in a marriage. I wasn't sure. I only knew it "rocked my world," so to speak because it created a new way of viewing the world as I knew it.

If someone had told me that "I hadn't seen anything yet," and that "my world was about to be rocked far more than I could have imagined," I would never have believed them. *What could possibly shake up my world more than what I had already gone through?*

I would be finding out soon enough.

CHAPTER 10

REMINISCING

My mind drifted back to age twelve.

Science lessons had subsided and we were waiting for the bell to ring. I must have been a sight. My broken front teeth revealed a tent-shaped hole in my smile. Not that I smiled too much at school, because I was extremely shy. My glasses usually were tipped on the bridge of my nose, because I spent time bending and twisting the arms to get them to feel better as they pressed against my head. Clothing hung loosely on my fully developed young body. If it were tight against me, it excited sensations that I not only didn't accept, but I did not yet understand their origin.

"Carrie, come over here," Mr. Bell, the teacher, invited eagerly.

Did he really just talk to me? I nervously thought.

"Carrie, I bet you're a good arm wrestler," he invited again.

His words WERE intended for me. I blushed.

I glanced across the room to where the hottest, most popular, muscular guys were arm wrestling each other. *He must be kidding*, I quickly decided.

"Carrie, I bet you can beat them all," Mr. Bell repeated.

I blushed again, but something stirred inside me. Not very many people took this much interest in me outside my family, I reflected.

"Carrie, aren't you a softball player?" Mr. Bell continued.

Did I tell him that? I don't remember, I thought. *Why was he being so persistent? He must really care about me*, I considered.

It became readily clear that Mr. Bell was not going to let up. By this time, all the boys were looking my way at my stringy-haired, skinny body, with the baggy clothing that hid my developing curves underneath. I had on a full, pleated skirt, with a short-sleeved shirt. Of course, it was not tucked in, to give me the comfort I sought.

One of the boys teased, "she can't beat us, are you kidding?"

"You might be surprised," Mr. Bell interjected.

OK, if he believes in me, I'll try it, I relinquished.

I sauntered bravely to where the boys were seated. *As long as the teacher is close by they won't make fun of me*, I realized.

"Go Carrie," Mr. Bell cheered, I heard loud and clear.

I smiled a closed-mouth smile. *This is kind of fun*, I thought. *I've got to win, I don't want to let Mr. Bell down*, I considered further.

I pressed hard. I strained. I pushed. I beat one boy after another as they were each defeated. I was declared victor over the guy with the huge muscles, the one that had been beating all the other guys. I was astonished, and pleased. I wonder how Mr. Bell had seen this in me? Had it been because of my good grades? I certainly didn't look muscular, I didn't think.

The boys looked surprised, embarrassed, and humbled. They never dismissed me again as the nobody that sat in the back of the room. There were the beginnings of a new spark of respect I felt from them.

That statement could not be made about my middle school days, in general. Name-calling occurred daily. Words were shoved at me like "ugly," "toothless," and everything in-between. I tried not to let it get to me, but it hurt all the same. The words stuck like flies on flypaper. I had been so traumatized from the root canals I had received the year prior, that I didn't want to pursue getting crowns. I didn't want anyone to touch my mouth for a very long time.

Who you are inside is what really counts, I held to. This stubbornness to claim that ideal is what kept me from making the changes that would have made my life easier. For years, that proclamation would be my only balm of comfort. I did not want to let it go.

What hurt the most was having Donald call me names. We crossed paths everyday at the bus stop, and since he only lived a few houses down, we saw each other in the neighborhood all the time. *He knows me the best, why does he have to call me names?* I wondered. *Someday I'll show him,* I plotted.

Life in my family stayed about the same. I don't remember being challenged to take better care of myself. Maybe they knew how hard it was in middle school and didn't want to make it harder on me. Or, maybe because I'm so stubborn, they had given up trying to reach me. *Surely they must know what kind of pain I'm living with,* I thought. I don't remember it being discussed.

My mind shifted back a year, where I sat restlessly in my 6th grade classroom. Spring was in the air, and it was hot and sticky. I didn't relish that about the Midwest climate. I sat with my legs crossed, swinging them in a rhythmic dance to ease the boredom I felt from sitting at length.

All at once there were sensations arising that I did not recognize. I squeezed tighter and the sensations became more intense. I continued swinging my legs more intensely.

"Stop. Stop that," Mrs. Sour bellowed across the room.

I continued swinging my legs, wondering what these new sensations were. I felt myself flush, and the sensations turned to tingles that traveled up my abdomen and arms. I no longer had a choice, as I obligingly followed the drive of these urges that were making themselves known.

"Stop," Mrs. Sour repeated.

Was she talking to me? Does she know what I'm doing? What am I doing, anyway? It must be something bad, as I considered that perhaps she really was talking to me. *She's not looking at me,* I further considered. I decided I better stop anyway.

That year Karen and I shared the same class. It had been the only year we shared the same teacher, even though we'd been at the same school since kindergarten. Karen rallied the girls in the classroom to each walk past my desk and either call me a name or make a face at me. I felt humiliated. *What had I done?* I believe now, that perhaps her jealousy of my good grades drove her behavior. I didn't know it at the time. I only knew that it hurt. I felt betrayed. She'd been my next door neighbor as far back as I could remember. I thought she was my best friend.

The put-downs lasted several weeks. For me, it felt like forever. Girls can be so mean.

Mrs. Sour (sometimes she WAS sour, according to the kids) asked me to step into the hallway with her. *Did she know what the girls were doing?* I wondered.

"Someday you're going to be someone great," she said to me. *Where did that come from?*

I pondered. *Did she just want to make me feel better because she heard what the girls were saying? Or, was it because I made the best grades in the class?* I tried to sort through all the reasons I could think of for her saying what she did.

Did she know something I didn't know about myself? I never knew the truth.

CHAPTER 11

STILL CLIMBING

"At 5:04 p.m. an earthquake struck the San Francisco Bay Area. It measured 6.9 on the Richter Scale. It is the worst earthquake that has occurred on the San Andreas Fault since the great nineteen hundred and six San Francisco earthquake."

I turned the news up louder. *Did I really hear what I thought I heard? It couldn't be! Mark worked in San Francisco!* I looked at my watch. It was 7:40 p.m. I watched on my television in Urbandale, Iowa, and quickly figured out the time, two hours earlier in California. Mark rented an apartment in the East Bay. *Had he made it home? Was he safe?* Questions flooded my mind faster than a speeding train. I ran to process all the information being thrust upon me.

It was October 17th, 1989.

I called him.

"Hello?" Mark questioned.

"Hi, I called to see if you were OK," I replied.

"Yea, I take BART and that is the safest place you can be. It even goes under the ocean, and they say an earthquake wouldn't hurt you inside the tube," Mark informed me.

"Really?" I queried.

"Yep, but these aftershocks are pretty hairy," he continued.

We continued a brief conversation before hanging up. The whole time we were talking, my mind became preoccupied with the idea that we were actually getting ready to move there. *Was I crazy?! What was I thinking?*

My mind continued trying to make sense of everything. We had already moved eight, or was it ten times by now? I had lost track. I had little energy left for boxing and unboxing, making address changes, and all the other details involved. Funny, he made the decisions to move, and I ended up with all the work. It became more and more difficult with the emotional, and now physical distance, between us. Where would I end up working? Would I be able to be a school counselor again? Questions popped into my brain like popcorn, unable to stop and find a place to rest. *At least I would be able to have another child, a girl, a companion for Erin.* I couldn't think about all of these things right now. I had too much to do. Where to start?

The house had sold just last week, and Mark flew back the following weekend, to help with the cross-country move. I dreaded saying good-bye to my family, yet another time. *At least there was a seemingly good reason; Mark's health. But wasn't that why we moved out this way? It was all a jumble. It must be the way Mark was feeling.*

I made loving choices towards him, in spite of feeling so depleted myself. It continued to be hard to remain open when I kept being wounded. The scars were becoming so deep that I lost touch with my own feelings. So, instead of feeling, I just did whatever needed to be done. I became a robot or a mannequin, without expression.

That is who I was now.

When it began to rain, I tried to find the sunlight. And when the road had bumps, I looked a little farther to find smooth pavement. When things weren't good in my marriage, I went inside myself to look for comfort, because I talked to no one about it. He convinced me more and more that I really couldn't please him and fulfill his expectations. I just wasn't able to "be" for him in the ways he thought I should.

I kept trying in spite of it all, because I didn't believe in divorce. In fact, the possibility never entered my mind. So for me, alternatives were nonexistent. *I just had to get it right.*

We joined Mark in his apartment in late October. He had not made a bad choice, really. *But how had he overlooked the fact that smoke from the apartment below would come in through our vents?* I hated breathing that. I hated it for Erin too. Sonoma, California was a beautiful area. I found that it felt more like home than the valley, with all the browned out areas. The lush green trees in the Bay Area reminded me more of the Midwest. It seemed an easier adjustment because of this. We quickly became part of another church group, where we both had connections from our college years. That was a comfort also.

When the aftershocks struck, that was not comforting! At first, I would run in and pick up Erin, even if she was sleeping, and run out the door and down the stairs. Mark just looked at me like I had gone nuts. *Couldn't it be a bigger one that would actually damage the roof or something?* I didn't want to take any chances. So, I kept leaving the building. Eventually, after a few weeks, they subsided. I sighed with relief.

Our finances were suffering more and more from all of our moves. This time finding a house did not come so easily, especially after taking a loss on our house in Iowa. The houses in the Bay Area were definitely much more expensive, and I wondered if we would be able to buy a house at all. Our standards had become higher when we were used to having nice, comfortable houses in the other places we had lived. Here in the Bay Area, people lived without garages, lived with two bedrooms, not three, many had little or no yard, and frequently houses were fifty years old or more. Ugh! I wanted it all. *I had it before. Why couldn't I have it now?!*

After a great deal of struggle and searching, we decided to enlist the support of an investment partner and purchase in Fairfield, California, where we could get more for our money. I wasn't crazy about the idea of a partner that would get half the equity when we sold, but it looked like the only way we could buy a house. Living in Fairfield became our way of holding onto the three bedroom, two bath, two car garage American dream that we weren't ready to let go of.

Erin approached the start of kindergarten, and it would mean I would have to drive her into Vacaville to get into a good school. It was a price I more than willingly paid.

By this time, Mark was working on completing his second master's degree, in computer technology. It seemed to suit him better than administration. He could work with computers, and less with people. He more easily secured positions in computer education, and became happier with his work. I began substituting, but within a year, found an opportunity to work as a school counselor again.

I felt very blessed to have this opportunity.

When we were settled, I raised the question of having another child. Mark became agitated at the suggestion. I reminded him of his promise. He reminded me of his health, and all the unknowns we faced. I told him that it was important to me. It also felt like my last chance in the baby department. I would be turning thirty-five. My days were really numbered now.

He consented, reluctantly.

I prayed.

How did I get so lucky to have the opportunity to share my pregnancy again, with a close friend? God really looked out for me. Sally, a church friend, announced that they were expecting, within a few weeks of our announcement. I was delighted. They also had another daughter that shared a friendship with Erin. Our families spent a lot of time together. Life shifted for the better.

Jim, Sally's husband, held the position of marriage and family therapist, and confronted Mark whenever he was "out of line." I felt supported by his interjections. Mark began looking at himself and his behavior in ways he'd never done before. Erin challenged him also. She grew and matured rapidly into a person of her own.

Sally and I were able to share a hospital room when our babies were born. Mark engaged in the preparations with me this time around. He attended childbirth preparation classes, along with Jim and Sally. Mark talked me through contractions when I endured labor, and even used a tennis ball on my spine when I went into back labor. I had a quadruple blessing because I delivered naturally, after having previously had a C-section with Erin, thanks to the mid-wife.

As it turned out, a parent from school became the attending nurse during labor. When she recognized me, I felt terribly embarrassed, but she turned out to be one of the most gentle people I had ever met.

I gave birth to Kayla in April, 1991. I prayed that we would have a daughter. We did indeed.

I also prayed that she would be a good balance to Erin's highly energetic personality. Even while I carried her, I could tell she was a gentle personality. She exuded a calmness about her from the time she was born. She blessed our family in a way that we needed. I thrilled to see Erin embrace her, and play the "big sister."

With her birth in April, it allowed me to enjoy a long summer with Kayla and Erin. In the fall, I worked only part-time as a school counselor, and spent my other mornings with Kayla, while Erin attended kindergarten. Another close friend, Tracy, offered to take care of Kayla while I worked. Again, blessings poured down from above. Everything seemed to be falling into place. In fact, I worked part-time as a counselor for many years, which proved to be some of the best work years of my adult life.

Kayla demonstrated her specialness, much like Erin. One time when Kayla was a few years older, I was playing in her room with her, and we were talking about death, because her Sunday School teacher had died. Kayla was barely talking, but commented, "her teacher would be coming back as a baby."

I asked her who told her that. Did her Sunday School teacher tell her?

Without batting an eye, she said, "No, it was God."

I was dumbfounded.

Being home more and taking Erin to dance and gymnastic classes was very rewarding.

Watching Kayla grow and develop through her babyhood was a treasure. I wanted it to continue like this forever. Kayla was pure love. She constantly offered lots of hugs and smiles. She, like Erin, made up her own songs and would fill up the house with joy. It made us forget to think of the hard times that were surely ahead of us.

We wanted to be a family.

We wanted to have normal problems.

We wanted to enjoy each other and take vacations.

So we decided to take a trip to Disneyworld in August 1992.

With two small children in an airplane, it made for a very long day. *It will be worth it*, I thought, as I struggled to change diapers in the small bathroom cubicle. Kayla, now fifteen months old, was no longer a small newborn. She cooperated which definitely made it easier.

Exhausted, we made it to the hotel.

On the first morning, the girls were awake early. Erin jumped up and down with excitement getting Kayla stirred up as well. After sitting for a full day of flights, they were anxious to get out and move around. I roused, got showered, and tried to entertain the girls while Mark still slept. He seemed more tired than usual lately.

I worried how his kidneys might be holding up.

I wondered if he worried about the same thing.

We did not talk about it. It loomed like an elephant in the room of forbidden subjects.

Couldn't he just muster up some strength now, since we were on vacation? Was he really this tired?!

It was 10:00 in the morning, which meant only 7:00 a.m. California time. But then the clock kept ticking, 11:00 a.m., and then 12:00 p.m. The girls and I found our way to the continental breakfast the hotel served. But they would soon be ready for lunch, and Disneyworld would be crowded. We had come all this way, we didn't want to miss anything! By 12:30 p.m. Mark got up, and boy was he grumpy!

I could tell this was not going to be the fun vacation I had hoped. He didn't look well, either.

I wasn't sure, but I think his face looked a little puffy. I didn't say anything. I didn't want to give him more reasons to worry.

Once we got to the park, all was forgotten. Erin had a blast, and kept Kayla in giggles. Even the brief rainstorms didn't dampen the girls' spirits. We stayed mostly in the kiddie section, which was okay, because neither Mark nor I were crazy about fighting with the kids to try and do a lot of the adult activities. We did manage to see a few shows.

Back at the hotel, every morning mimicked the day before. It became a battle getting Mark up and moving. Not only was his energy level low, he continued getting grumpier by the second.

Our enjoyment of the vacation was circumvented by his mood. It only worsened when we returned home. When he went to the doctor, he discovered that the last of his kidney function had retreated. He now had to decide what kind of dialysis treatment he would endure. He chose peritoneal, which is an in-home method, so he would not have to drive anywhere, and could continue working. It meant ordering supplies to be delivered to our home, lots of supplies.

That fell to me.

I will never forget the first time the delivery truck pulled into our driveway. Box after box showed up, and filled the space inside our garage. How many boxes would he need? I asked, "Why so many?"

The answer I got was, "This is only one month's worth."

My mouth fell, frozen wide open.

Mark and I were equals in one respect, our determination. He kept working. When he came home, he collapsed on the floor. Kayla, oblivious, would fall on him, hugging and kissing him.

He adored it. I could not be that for him, because of the still-constant rejection. I kept plugging along, ordering his supplies, and assisting him with the dialysis.

His anger had turned to rage, and Erin and I tried to keep our distance. Erin would run into the room excited, ready to share something she'd made at school, and he would push her away, saying, "Move." She would be crushed, and end up in a heap on the couch. I tried to be the go-between, to ease her suffering.

There were times he would go in and wake Erin up out of a deep sleep. She would start crying, and I would say, "Why are you doing that?!" He only laughed. He continued being mean and hardened. We could not break through. He was consumed only by surviving his everyday world, and keeping the dialysis going.

He asked more and more of me. He wanted me to give him injections that were intended to build up his energy. He didn't want to have to go to the doctor's office to get shots each week, so asked if

I would do it for him. I waivered, being very nervous. I had my issues with him, but I didn't want to injure him with a needle! I complied, however, after seeing how difficult it was for him to function. I sought my friend, Sally, to give me mini-lessons on how to give injections.

Even so, when I gave him a shot, I half-closed my eyes and shoved it in the direction of his arm.

I hated doing that. I was not a nurse.

He needed it, so I did it.

At night, Kayla wailed in pain with ear infections. I was getting up frequently to take care of her. At night, Mark paced the floor, ranting. Other times, he alternated between raging and pacing. Still other times, he would fall into a mound on the floor, completely distraught.

Thankfully, most of these occurrences were after the girls had gone to bed.

He slept very little.

Neither did I.

After he'd been on dialysis for three months or so, he had a dialysis machine brought into our home. This allowed him to have dialysis during the night. He paced the floor even more, and I slept even less. The whir of the machine, in combination with Kayla's ear infections, thrust me into a zombie-like state. We were now both zombies in a bad horror movie. The girls helped to maintain some kind of normalcy in our lives. I had to keep meal and bedtime routines going for them. I feared failing them because I no longer had much left to give.

I was a dry well in a forsaken desert, and getting thirstier by the second.

CHAPTER 12

NOT SO SWEET SIXTEEN

The ceiling held a mishmash of hidden pictures and designs. I studied it carefully as I struggled to go to sleep. How long had I lain here? Two hours? Maybe three? I didn't know. I only knew that every night it became an inner battle to succumb to the slumber that regularly escaped me.

I drifted back to my English class, my junior year in high school. What story did we read? "Silent Snow, Secret Snow," read the title, by Conrad Aiken. I understood it perfectly because my world felt the same. The story told of a boy who felt more and more distant and withdrawn from his world. Analogies were made of his feelings to daydreams of snow. Mrs. Pinney, the teacher, wrote, "excellent insight into the story," on the paper I'd written.

Perhaps identifying with the story revealed a darker side of me that few people knew about, I thought. I spent an abundant amount of time in bed, and then I couldn't sleep once I got there.

Mostly I stared into space, feeling numb. *What had happened to me?* The counselor described it as depression. I just knew that everything had grown harder. Getting up to go to school felt painful. I no longer wanted to see my friends much. When I did get together with them, I related as a hollow shell. When I laughed, it felt empty, not really connected to the rest of me.

Images of days past flashed before me. Leaning against the railing to the school entrance, I displayed my new shoes, gold suede, with black leather accents. It took a lot of courage to be one of the first to promote a new fashion trend. *In 8th grade courage flowed easier than it does now*, I remembered. Thinking about it now, it struck me as humorous that me, of all people, would be the one to lead the way.

Of course little did I know that I would be the first. Not until I stood against the stair railing did it occur to me that this might be the case. Suddenly, all eyes were on me and my shoes. I gulped. *Great, I thought, just what I need, to have more reasons to get ostracized.* Then kids started pointing at my shoes, and then there were snickers rippling amongst the on-lookers. The gut-wrenching distress of that moment seared through me with the same intensity as if I had actually gone back in time.

Those moments and others like it, lived within me as if they were real. *Would they ever go away?* I pondered. The bus rides were the worst. With no way to escape, the looks and rejection had to be endured for the long forty-five minute ride home. I looked out the window and pretended not to exist. I just wanted life to get easier.

That looks like a spider, with hairy legs, I noticed, as I continued observing the shapes and images on the ceiling.

My mind wandered back to happier times last summer. My friend Marsha taught me to play guitar. I'd already been playing the piano for eight years, although I hated the routine of practicing. I oftentimes moved the timer forward when I thought I could get away with it. "Thirty minutes of practice," Mrs. Grushman kept saying, "no less."

My mom reinforced it at home as well. "We are paying for these lessons, and you need to do your part by practicing," she had said.

I complied, but it grew tiresome, nonetheless. There were so many other things I would rather be doing, like reading, or playing catch, or running around outside.

I had to admit that I really enjoy sitting down and playing the piano now. I'm glad that my mom made me stick with it, because otherwise I wouldn't be able to play like I do.

It had been my fantasy, though, to learn to play guitar. I'd taken a few lessons the prior year but it wasn't enough to help me play well. "Everyone develops their own style," the teacher had emphasized.

"What the heck did that mean?" I puzzled.

Marsha is the one that helped me figure it all out. "You can pick or you can strum, depending upon what kind of sound you want, and what you're most comfortable with," she explained.

She spent time with me going through camp songs and giving me the words and chords to take home so I could practice. I found guitar resonated with me, and that I discovered ways to figure out picking patterns. I practiced. I sang.

I made up songs.

I loved it.

Uncle Don and his family visited in late September. Engrossed in playing cards in the kitchen, I didn't think I could be heard in the family room, with the door closed. When I finished and stepped out, he said, "Was that you playing and singing? I thought it must have been the radio." I was flattered. *Did I really sound that good?*

Songwriting became one of my loves, along with playing the guitar. The guitar accompanied me to college, along with my other prized possessions. It never made me famous, but it kept me company and became an outlet for expressing myself.

Again my attention drifted back to the room and the awareness that I still had not drifted to sleep. My mind continued wandering. *How had I gotten to be depressed?*

My mind fluttered around the idea that perhaps the name-calling and rejection I had experienced had finally gotten to me. I'm going to ask Mom and Dad if I can get my teeth crowned, I considered. It's not worth all the turmoil I've gone through. Yes, who we are inside is most important, but maybe we have to take care of ourselves to allow others to see our inner beauty.

The following morning I found myself in Dr. Gizmo's office.

"I've decided to ask if I can get crowns on my teeth," I was telling the psychotherapist.

"Oh, what made you decide that?" he asked, in a monotone voice.

"I think I've been depressed partly because of all the name-calling and rejection I've been dealing with," I told him.

"I thought it didn't matter to you," he reflected.

"I decided that it does matter," I said, "I don't want to keep hurting."

The room grew silent. *Why did he always just sit there looking down at me with those silly little round glasses sitting at the end of his nose?* I entertained myself.

The silence made me uncomfortable. *What could I say to fill the silent space?* Guess I'll just keep talking.

"After I decided to ask about the crowns, I've been feeling better," I continued. "It's been a really long time since I've seen myself without broken teeth. I looked at myself in the mirror the other day and realized that I don't look that bad, if you look past the teeth."

"Oh yea?" he responded. *Couldn't he say more than that? Couldn't he say something positive?* I shifted in my chair. *Now I really felt bare and vulnerable. I didn't like feeling this way.*

"I think I'll start curling my hair, and maybe my parents will let me get contacts so I won't have to wear glasses anymore," I revealed.

"Do you think those things will help you feel better?" he probed.

"Yes, in high school everything is about looks and I'm ready to make myself fit in more. I think I can do it and not lose myself now," I stated thoughtfully.

"How will you do that?" he questioned me.

"I don't know, I'll just have to figure it out as I go," I continued.

There was another silence. *He's making me uncomfortable*, I thought again. *I don't think I like him. I only came to see him because my parents had insisted.* I think I scared them when I started sleeping a lot. *Maybe I could stop seeing Dr. Gizmo too*, I secretly pondered.

A plan began to form in my mind. *I'll fix myself up and then I'll show Donald. He'll never call me a name or make fun of me again*, I thought, with the conviction of one fully intending to implement a new blueprint.

I was ready for a new blueprint for living.

CHAPTER 13

THE VIEW AT THE TOP

My place no longer positioned itself on the frontlines, carrying the flag of martyrdom. Ready to unfurl the banner of surrender, I wanted to join the infirmary, to find a place to heal my wounded heart. I was totally and completely exhausted, physically, mentally, and emotionally.

Thank goodness for my strong spirit. Thank you God, for holding onto me, albeit by a thread.

In this state, I prayed like I have never prayed before, or since. I hurt more than ever. And I felt totally alone. I felt too much shame to reach out to friends for help. I felt shame for the rage that was a regular part of our home. I felt embarrassed and empty. I struggled to find meaning in my life. I prayed for angels to watch over us. One night I swear I saw a bright light outside our bedroom window, that rolled open, and then would retreat into a ball. The light shone brilliantly, so I had to squint, and still, had a hard time looking directly at it. I didn't see a being, but could this be the angel, or a being of light that I prayed for? I wasn't sure, but it gave me hope where there was none.

When we moved to Sonoma, back in 1989, I was approached by a Mary Kay consultant, and she convinced me to sell cosmetics. It gave us a little extra income, but what it gave me held even more value. It helped me to begin building my strength by acquiring skills in restoring my self-esteem. I developed more self-confidence, as I listened to motivational speakers who talked about believing in yourself and thinking the very best. In my counseling job, I taught self-esteem building skills to young children, and I found that it indirectly built up my self-esteem also. I needed all I could get. I could feel myself losing it.

At night, for years now, Mark would engage me in making love, by touching me to arousal. When I became responsive, he would spout, "forget it, you're not worth it," and storm out of the room. Another frequent scenario included him chanting, "Say f***, say it, say it!"

When I refused, he would get up and leave. In both situations, he would seek out his video harem. I felt like a mouse inside a large cage, hiding in the corner. I didn't dare come out to play.

I started doing more things for myself out of necessity. I had a balloon valence I had wanted to hang on the kitchen window. I had never hung a curtain by myself before. I climbed up on the counter with grit and determination, and decided I was going to figure out how to do it. I accomplished the task, but not without angst. It started me thinking. How many other things did I depend on Mark to do? It scared me when I started to stare my reliance in the face. The reality hit me; I was, indeed, co-dependent. I noticed an ad in the newspaper for group meetings based upon the book *Co-dependent No More*, by Melody Beattie.

What did that mean, exactly? I wasn't sure, even with all my counseling background. I wanted to find out. I had to take care of myself, for the girls' sake. I started attending workshops.

I could barely find my way out of our neighborhood, let alone anywhere else. Mark always drove. My sense of direction was lacking. I started learning how to use MapQuest, and printed out the directions and stuck them in my glove box. When a repairman entered our home, I watched closely to observe his work. I forced myself to use tools from the garage. I took a computer class, because Mark did all the computer work in our home. I relied totally upon him for anything that we needed that way too.

Something else that occurred during this time was that I was called to the priesthood in my church. In the Mission of Christ Church, women were not traditionally part of those responsibilities until very recent years. In order to consider the call, I had to accept my worth, not only as a person of value, but as a woman who had something to offer. Mark had a hard time with the idea of me "joining the ranks with him," since he already held a priesthood office. I tried to separate myself more, and make my own decision. In accepting the call, I found myself taking a giant step towards reclaiming myself. I didn't know it at the time.

As the darts of rage continued to hurl, I continued to find ways to make peace in our home.

Whenever he wanted to watch TV, I didn't ask to watch something that I wanted. I didn't know how to operate the recorder, so I went without. That would be something I would learn later.

When the radio played, I relinquished choosing the channels, because I didn't want the conflict.

With every decision I made, I began a slow death of myself, a gradual disappearance of my essence.

The integrity of my being began eroding. I completely lost touch with who I was. I didn't see it coming, and I didn't do it consciously, but it just began to happen. In the process of making peace with him in our home, I lost peace with myself. I laughed without my heart really being in it. I developed a shell of armor to protect myself. The less I showed of my internal self, the less he could reject, and the less I hurt. The more I pleased him and did what he wanted, the less pain I endured. The more I tried to become someone else that I wasn't, the more that I didn't even know who I was anymore.

There were no more tears.

Tough soldiers don't cry.

I became more and more lonely. I was lost to myself, and more and more out of touch with the world around me, because I related more and more as a shell of a person and not as the vibrant alive person that had gotten buried underneath. My heart was locked. Not even I could find the key.

It was June 1993.

Erin had endured her share of pain along with me. Kayla still seemed unaffected, although I wondered. Erin came to me one evening and said, "Mommy, it's like I'm looking out the window and it's all foggy, and the curtain is torn."

What a profound thing for my six year old to be saying.

She continued with, "When is it all going to end?"

In all the infinite wisdom I could muster, I countered with, "I don't know, but I'm here for you. You know you can always count on me."

"It just hurts so much," she said.

"I know, Erin, I know." My heart was bleeding profusely.

In July 1993, Mark found himself on the floor crying out, "I can't take it any more. I can't do this, I want it to be over." I watched helplessly. His rage kept him isolated from my comfort. I didn't know what to do.

I wanted it to be over too.

Late on one of those early July nights, Mark came into the bedroom where I was sleeping and reached over and slugged me on the arm, awakening me out of a deep slumber. In my dazed, semi-conscious dream state, I was not fully awake. As I struggled to awaken, I saw in my mind's eye, a vision. In the vision, I could see myself being dragged on the ground behind Mark, with a white cord connected between us. In the instant he struck me, I heard a snap in my mind, and I saw the cord snap, and at a deep soul level, I felt a snap. In that moment, I thought, "Damn it, I really tried! This is it!" I didn't know what the "it" was, but on a really deep level it felt like the end of our marriage. *I could take no more.*

The next morning my arm ached. It served as a reminder of what had happened the night before. This was real. I confronted Mark. I said, "You hit me last night."

He said, "What are you talking about?"

I said, "You know what I'm talking about. My arm hurts because you hit me. I was asleep and you woke me up by hitting me."

He laughed, "So what if I did?"

I fumed. The steam started rising until a cloud formed overhead. The loud thunder in my head screamed the truth of my life. *I was married to someone who did not treat me right.*

The truth of those words stretched out right in front of me. There were no more confusing words or behaviors to sort through. It was as plain as the nose on my face.

He hit me.

This was real.

I could no longer deny it, or smooth it over. The truth was undeniable. It was not even close to loving, and it was not okay. Pure and simple. No longer would I be treated like this!

The thunder had only begun to roll!

CHAPTER 14

THE UNRAVELING

The dream. The memory of the steep stairway came flooding back with full force, following the vision. The memory of the dream I had in college returned to me as if it had just happened yesterday. I knew it was true. *I also knew in an instant that as I had climbed the stairs, it had been my life with my husband of these past fourteen years. I also knew, with certainty, that I was at the top of the stairs.* Nothing else was clear, but the pure truth of these thoughts tingled through my being, leaving not even a trace of doubt.

Another thing that happened at the same time was that I lost all control of myself and my carefully monitored emotions. I had been very much in control of myself and my life. As I felt pain and disappointment with the way things went in my marriage, I carefully monitored myself so that I still could make things okay, or try to make them at least appear that way. *We were supposed to keep trying to make things work. We were a family.* I hadn't believed in divorce.

I kept trying no matter what. But when he hit me, I no longer felt in control of all those emotions that had been accumulating, and hidden away.

When I snapped, it felt as if my heart was bursting wide open, and I could no longer hold it closed. I became awake to the experience of life all over again. However, I awakened first to the pain, which I had been numb to for so long. It was intense, agonizing pain, which lasted for many months. Pain, and the awareness of the many losses I had suffered, created a deep permeating sadness, grief, and anger, which was relentless.

I started pushing back. Where there had once been a puppy that learned to roll over and play dead, now a terrier appeared, beginning to growl.

I also began falling apart.

I started having nightmares. I became a spewing fountain, gushing forth with emotion that I didn't even know I possessed. It was a very tumultuous time for me. My brain was a hodgepodge of dissidence, trying to put together a puzzle that made some sort of sense. My life had not been what I believed. I needed to tell my story over and over. I needed to cry and feel and experience all those things that I hadn't allowed myself, because it had all been submerged for so long.

There were weeks and months of flashbacks as one painful memory after another returned to haunt my days and nights and reveal their truths; as acts of injustice. Along with it came hurt and anger towards Mark, and towards myself. *Why had I not seen it sooner?* These experiences pervaded my being and became my reality.

It was during this time that I began seeing a therapist. I realized that Mark's rage had now infused me, so that it was no longer just his problem, but now mine as well. I continued to search and to pray. I read and studied everything I could get my hands on, trying to understand what was happening. I wanted to figure out how to somehow make these experiences and feelings go away. *Could there be a way to smooth over all the past pains and hurts and trials and still be married?*

Desperation would sum up what I felt during this time in my life.

I went to see my therapist.

"Dr. Lewis, I feel like I'm having a nervous breakdown. I'm losing all control. I cry all the time. It seems the waterworks won't stop. My nights are plagued by nightmares that terrorize me. My days are infused with flashbacks. I'm scared."

"Carrie, what you are experiencing is Post Traumatic Stress Disorder. It should get better with time, but you have a lot of re-living of the past to do, before you can get back in balance."

At least I felt affirmed to know that what I was going through had a name, especially when it filled every corner of my existence. It was not going way. It was here to stay, and everything I encountered attested to that fact.

"Carrie, it feels like you need to sing," Dr. Lewis tentatively suggested.

That was exactly the way I felt! She'd hit the nail right on the head. I NEED TO SING.

I needed to open myself up. It all wanted to come busting out. Desperation was calling to express myself from the depths of my being. Singing was a perfect way to do that!

When I went to Kaiser to pick up Mark's medications, I found myself in an overly crowded waiting room. In spite of the long line of waiting individuals, they called my name to come to the front of the line. I obliged. A pharmacist came from the back and greeted me with, "Why didn't you tell us that the medication you were picking up needed to be refrigerated?!" I was confounded. *He was asking ME?! Wasn't HE the pharmacist*?! I felt shame and humiliation to have him yelling at me for no reason.

Everyone in the room looked at me with disdain, as if I carried some horrible contagious disease.

I wasn't even the sick one.

Another time I went to Burlington Coat Factory to pick up some work clothes for Mark. It was hard for him to get out and he needed a larger size because peritoneal dialysis left his abdomen larger from all the fluid he had to carry around. I returned home with the items and discovered they weren't the right size, after all. I went back to the store to return them and found that they didn't accept returns. I yelled at the store clerk. *Who was this? I didn't usually behave this way!*

I even scared myself.

On a different day, I was driving home and got ready to exit the freeway, when my car ran out of gas. _Thank goodness the girls were not with me._ I eased over to the very narrow shoulder, where construction work had been taking place. Beyond the shoulder, there were eighteen inch ruts which had been created by enormous caterpillar tires working in previously wet soil.

Wearing heels, I awkwardly tackled the ridges and valleys of these deep troughs, to get to the gas station. I cried, not crocodile tears, but elephant tears, because they were enormous and would have filled the ruts my shoes were tracing, if the valves had been turned on full-force. But I showed some restraint, after all, I would soon be face to face with the gas attendant. _How had I gotten into this mess?_ My brain no longer worked normally for me.

Every week I would spend an hour in the driveway, breaking down boxes for the recycling bin. Remember all those boxes that were being delivered for dialysis? Now I was breaking them apart. I should have gotten some kind of award to so religiously participate in this weekly ritual.

I think in a way, it provided a soothing balm for my weary body, to stand in one place and mechanically engage in such a mindless act. It enabled me to step out of the tension that was inside the house. It gave me a chance to think. I could just breathe. It added to my isolation, however.

Not one neighbor even noticed or stepped out to say, "Hey, how are you doing?"

It only added to my loneliness.

During this time I felt extremely vulnerable and needy. I didn't have a shoulder to cry on. I was still too embarrassed to talk to my friends about what was happening to me. My parents and my sister were the best listening ears there were, even from afar. I hesitated to dump too much on them. They had their own stuff to deal with.

I felt like I already had taken up more than my share of time at the confessional booth.

Who would be there to listen?

CHAPTER 15

TOUCHED BY AN ANGEL

It was late July in 1993.

We went to church camp in beautiful Santa Cruz, California. The massive grounds were filled with the sounds of birds and rushing water from the wide creek, covered by a quaint wooden bridge. Majestic redwood trees lined the area, with delicate, sprawling ferns underneath.

Trails led into the hills that cradled the intimate space, which was cherished by attendees. I'd grown to love this place. We had been attending camps here for the past twelve years, since moving to California. I looked forward to the annual family camp all year long.

It was a healing environment for our family.

Mark spent a lot of time playing cards with friends. I spent a lot of time chasing after the girls. Kayla was still very little and in diapers. I spent time going back and forth from the nursery. I felt extremely exhausted, but I kept marching forward. My friend Jerry helped in the nursery quite often. I found myself being very grateful for his supportive presence. I also was very aware that I was highly attracted to him. I tried to keep some distance, because I knew "my cord was dangling," and looking for a place to reside. I felt very unmarried, yet I did not want my family to be disrupted.

I was highly conscious that I was, indeed, still married whether I felt it or not.

He expressed compassion for me, knowing the illness Mark endured, seeing my struggle looking after the girls by myself. I felt compassion in return, knowing that his wife had died many years earlier, and he had been a single dad for a long time. We shared a few glances, a few brushes past each other.

That was all it took.

Jerry had been a Marine Biologist before his wife passed away. Since that time he had been spending his time and energy engaged in saving coastal marine life, maybe at some level trying to bring back a piece of her. His tall, muscular physique would have been enough to catch my attention, but it was his smooth, tan skin, deep hazel eyes, and dark wavy hair that took my breath away. His gentle words and tender glances captured my heart and wouldn't let go.

It was too late.

Over the years I'd tried so hard not to look at other men, let alone be attracted to one. The last chip of ice in the corner of my heart melted away. My mind and heart became intertwined with his, and against the voice of reason, the rescue flag waved in his direction. Yes, I wanted him to be my shining knight and whisk me away to where life was simpler and worry free. I wanted my pain to disappear into a mist of ecstasy. My fantasy included being wrapped in his warm, inviting embrace in a place where there was no illness, no pain, and no heart-rending decisions that needed to be made.

In a letter he wrote to me soon after camp, he revealed that he felt the same way. He visited me in my dreams. He inhabited my daydreams. His energy accompanied me throughout the day. In these ways, he never left my side.

However, he was miles from where I lived, and we were in two different worlds. My real world remained the same, with the tough decisions I was faced with. I was still married to someone who could not embrace me the way Jerry was doing.

Jerry and I had, indeed, fallen in love with each other. *Now what?* My heart had been unleashed, and chosen a different nest in which to roost. It was one of those other things that I did not have control over. For fourteen long years I had dwelled in the desert of discontent. Now I was being allured into an oasis where I could soak in pure admiration. Like a starving child, I chased after crumbs of acceptance. I could not resist. There were letters and phone calls, of which Mark was not aware. My heart opened up to him about my pain and the burdens I'd carried in my marriage.

My life had now become more complicated, not simpler. But it felt wonderful. Instead of only trudging through pain each day, I delighted in fantasies of being in grassy meadows near where he was on the coast, among wildflowers in the open air. He shared the same sentiments in his letters, and occasionally in a stolen phone call. He spoke about his pain in being alone, and the challenges of being a single dad. We clung to each other's heartfelt embraces.

I did not want to hurt Mark. I was only trying to survive.

The communication from Jerry included not only affirmations, but prods and challenges to keep doing what I could to heal my family and marriage. Thank goodness there was a long physical distance between Jerry and me. The temptation to meet may have been too enticing.

Jerry helped me to love myself and restore my confidence in ways I hadn't been able to, for a very long time. In the process, I began to get glimpses of what a relationship could be like. I started remembering what it had been like with Rick, from college. So, in my naivety, and in my despair, I continued to let the relationship grow, so that I could continue to function in the ways I needed at home. Jerry restored faith in me as a desirable woman. He was the anchor in the ongoing storm of my life.

The longer we maintained communication, the harder it became because we wanted to be together. He needed someone nearby to be part of his everyday world. I could not let go of my marriage until I had given it a full shot. I knew that being wrapped up in Jerry did not help.

I still did not believe in divorce. I had to let go and set him free of the emotional ties we had developed. He needed to end our communication and find someone to meet all of his needs in a more realistic relationship. I felt eternally grateful to him.

He restored my life.

Mark received his transplant in the fall of 1993. He was grateful and went through a transformation in some ways, with a new appreciation for life, but he still had a lot of his own healing to do with his emotions.

So there were more storms to be weathered.

When I went to visit him in the hospital, I accidentally bumped his foot. His foot was very sensitive, and felt numb, he said. He yelled at me. I had to leave the room, because I felt I couldn't endure anymore. I remember going around the corner in the hallway, looking out the window, with tears falling down my cheeks. *How much more pain could I endure?*

He and I were both in therapy at this time in our lives, both separately and together. Mark showed a renewed motivation and interest in me and bent over backwards to try and regain my trust. I was slow to respond. I needed him to hear my pain and understand the lonely roads I had been walking with him. His tolerance for listening was still very limited. He wanted me to "get over it." *How did I "get over" sixteen years of pain, and simply erase the chalkboard? The bigger question for me became, how did I reconnect the loose cord of my heart that no longer was connected to him?*

Funny, the sexual relationship had improved between Mark and me, because Jerry opened my heart to my tender self. I was very aware, though, of the source of my new awakening. Mark was aware too, of my emotional absence, and the connection that existed between Jerry and me.

During this time, Mark kicked into full gear, trying to "win me over." He entered a radio contest for free tickets to a dinner/dance party. He won. He took me on a bay dinner cruise. He wrote notes and planned creative dates to allure me. I can't say I didn't enjoy the attention, it's just that it was very hard to trust that his actions were sincere.

He knocked on the door of my heart and there was no answer. No one was home.

There were still so many hurtful memories. I held a lot of pain and anger. Forgiveness dangled in a narrow passageway, with no access. I felt I had far surpassed the seven times seventy pardon limit of which the Bible speaks. I continued to try with everything in me. I wanted my family to be whole.

We attended a Catholic marriage clinic, called Retrouvaille. It had been recommended by some acquaintances, who had found it helpful. Sally and Jim came to our rescue by watching the girls for the weekends, which allowed us to participate in the overnight intensive program. In a series of several weekends, we participated in guided journaling back and forth for couples that were in the danger zone. We realized that we were in that category. I was willing to try anything that could salvage what was left of our marriage. During these weekends we cautiously shared gut-wrenching truths with each other.

He found I would not be a quick-fix. I found that the feelings were just not being resurrected.

On the way home after one of the weekends, we were discussing whether we would be able to work things out. Mark commented, "Well, neither one of us would be leaving, so we'll still be in the marriage, but I don't know if you can fulfill me."

That night I had another nightmare. In it, I was running down the hall with someone chasing close behind me. I felt in the dream that this person wanted to murder me. I went into the garage, where a figure with long hair and glasses looked down at a child lying on the pavement, dead and bleeding. I woke up in a panic. My understanding at the time was that that's how I would feel staying in the marriage, that perhaps the child in me would, or already, had died. *Could the dead child be our marriage?*

If only I could just release a plug to my brain, drain it out, and go on my merry way.

If only it was that easy . . .

CHAPTER 16

LETTER TO MARK

February 7, 1995

Dear Mark,

I thought I should write to you about some thoughts that are on my mind. I have prayed for help to "open up my blocks," and I can feel it happening this morning. You know, the reason that I've had to wrestle with talks I've given at church is because I've had such a hard time getting to my deeper self lately. It's related to sharing in sermons, but it's also related to sharing with you, because as I've wrestled, I've been able to get to that deeper part of me, and in turn, share it with you now.

Let me try to explain it so you can understand. During the years that you were suppressing parts of yourself, and coping by being angry, etc., I suppressed parts of myself, and coped in my own ways. One of the biggest ways that I coped was by squelching my desires and my needs. I don't blame you for this. It was a mutually satisfying arrangement. You asserted what you wanted, where you wanted to go, and I went along for the ride and did not disagree so that I could stay married, and not feel like a failure. I also lived for the glimmers of hope that I occasionally felt, that you really did love me, and could show it in the ways I needed. Many of the changes you've seen in me in the past year or so are the blossoming of those needs and desires that have previously been pushed under.

They are very important parts of who I am. Yes, I am growing a lot as an individual. I really, really need to keep moving forward. It doesn't have to go against "us," not if you try and understand, and give me the support and freedom I need. I'm not asking for freedom to be alone and independent, as you think. It's come out that way, because of my struggle to get in touch with what has been happening inside me. As I said, I really have to struggle to get down to my deeper self. I developed such an in-grained habit of coping for so long, by denying myself, that it's hard to get in touch with it now, and be honest.

There's still that part of me that wants to keep pushing myself under to "make everything work out." When I sense that by sharing myself conflict is created, or that by being honest, it means going our separate directions, my automatic learned response is to push it underground. I guess I've felt that I've tried to share all these things that I'm sharing now, during the past year, and I hit roadblocks with you. So, I guess since these are the same things that keep coming up in me, I'm trying again, with new words, in an attempt to help you understand.

One of the specific things I'm talking about is my drive to read and understand spiritual principles. That is one of the parts of me that I suppressed for many years. Sure I prayed a lot during those years, but it wasn't for my spiritual growth. The prayers were usually prayers of desperation and pleading. Through those many years I understood, at a gut level, much of what relationships are about, and what perhaps could be. The longings that you feel now, such as wanting me to touch you, and wanting to "merge" spiritually and emotionally with you, are the longings that I felt over and over for many, many years.

In spite of your rejection of me, and in spite of my own pain and longing, I was very loyal to you in every sense of the word. I never even put you down in my conversations with others. I fought even to protect you from others seeing the angry, disgruntled self that you showed me at home. I did this for you (which probably was not the best thing for you in the long run), but probably mostly for my own preservation and image. I wanted others to believe that everything was okay with us. I also felt protective of your church image, and your priesthood.

After coping this way for so long, and with the knowledge I gained from the co-dependency group I attended, I felt like an exploding pressure cooker. Everything from the past sixteen years started coming out. It began, I think, when I started "yelling back." Then I knew I was in trouble, that your problem had become mine, especially when I started steaming at other people about you. That's when I started seeing a counselor.

I've had some new insight regarding my dream about the staircase. I believe the heaviness that I felt climbing the stairs was in not feeling accepted for who I was, and in not feeling the freedom to be who I was, because instead, I was absorbed with making you my project. For example, leading you to emotional health, taking care of your physical needs during your illness, and supporting you in your career changes. After your transplant, since you've taken on helping yourself more, that has given me freedom to let go of being responsible for you, and explore more of who I am and what makes me happy.

Being free of burdens and fulfilling more of my own needs and desires is what signifies my joyful state, with outstretched arms at the top of the stairs. It feels good. I will never again be the person that I was. I have to continue growing, rapidly maybe, for awhile. I think eventually I'll catch up with myself and slow down. I need interactions with other people for my growth. One of my ways of coping during the "trying years" was to shut myself off from other people, especially other men, because I think at some level I knew how vulnerable I was, and I was afraid of being drawn to someone else. I was willing to save our marriage at all costs, even to my own suffering and harm.

I'm no longer willing to push my needs aside. In fact, emotionally, I'm incapable of it. It's kind of like our friend Jim's mother, who started putting her foot down and remodeling her house, by asserting herself like crazy because she hadn't done it in the past in her marriage. She and Tim are closer now, I think because she's been able to assert herself more and be more present in their relationship. I left my emotions in the back seat for such a long time, that now they are demanding to be in the driver's seat.

I don't feel as closed off from other people. I feel much freer to interact and I don't worry about whether the other person is a male or female. It feels good to not be afraid of other people and to risk getting to know them. Do you remember how highly anxious I used to be?! I think I've grown a lot in this respect.

You've asked a lot about Jerry. I think the meaning that I attached to relating to him was that he became symbolic of "the accepted and thus, freed self" that I felt in relation to him. I'm grateful to him, that through the acceptance I felt from him, I was able to re-discover some of the buried parts of myself.

In spite of our bad times, I have grown a lot with you. I'm eternally grateful to you for encouraging me to pursue teaching and to encourage me outside of my shy self. In spite of hating our many moves, we've had a lot of experiences and I've grown in ways I never would have, and I wouldn't trade those experiences for anything. I like who I've become. I guess there were times when I really didn't like myself, either, or I wouldn't have always put you before me.

You've said that you want to know the key to my heart. I guess the key is in loving and accepting me, consistently and in all ways, and giving me the freedom to discover me, and continue growing in the ways that I need and desire, so that I can find the joy at the top of the staircase.

Do I love you? I do. Do I love you in passionate, romantic ways? I have felt it in moments when I have seen the tender, gentler you. I have felt it in moments when I've caught glimpses of your hairy, muscular body. I've also felt it in moments when you've extended yourself to me. I know there have been times recently when you've gone out of your way, or you were really thinking just of me. Perhaps these things are part of the key to re-awakening more passion within me. You know, I also believe that a satisfying sexual relationship comes after other things are in order, such as security and acceptance for each of us.

Well, there you have it, an honest appraisal of who I am and where I am. Maybe you can soak it in on your way back home, and respond to it this weekend. I want there to be an "us" and for us to be a family, but maybe you don't like who I'm becoming, or where I'm going, wherever you seem to think that is.

Drive carefully.

Love,
Carrie

CHAPTER 17

THE COLLAPSE

Water was rising to my knees. I sank deeper, hanging onto a pole, as the wind whirled around me. I grappled to hold on, as the water kept rising higher and higher. It was another dream intruding upon my sleepless nights. It was reflective of the intense emotions I coped with.

The dream I struggled with the most, however, was the one I'd had back in college, of climbing the stairs. I consumed many hours journaling, searching for understanding that so easily eluded me. I spent lots of time pondering the meaning of these things. Much of that time was spent in the yard, while I gardened.

While Mark spent many angry years, I retreated more and more into the yard to find refuge.

I enjoyed being close to the earth, planting, pruning, and nurturing whatever was in front of me. I suppose it came from my Native American background. I learned that my great, great, great grandmother was a full-blooded Cherokee. I wondered whether her spirit was present with me still. I thought of this sometimes while I worked outside.

I also thought about Jerry. What was he doing? Had he moved on and found someone to love? Were the wildflowers in bloom? It was still so hard letting go. I thought of him when I saw the red-winged blackbirds in the hills as I drove the girls to school. It always seemed like they were there just to greet me each morning. Did Jerry see red-winged blackbirds where he lived?

When my own rage erupted, I again retreated to the yard. This time, I uprooted old juniper bushes that I had always thought were an eyesore anyway. This required me to dig a good eighteen to twenty-four inches into the ground. No problem. I had lots of energy to let out. I was determined to not let my anger erupt at the girls. I replanted flowering primrose bushes, and then enjoyed watching them bloom. We had a small palm tree in our front yard, with a circular planter surrounding it. I delighted in planting wildflowers that would surprise me with their blooms. This made me feel close to Jerry. Rose bushes, however, absorbed the greater part of my time, with pruning, pruning, and more pruning. They ran the full length of the side of the house, and they sure were beautiful in full bloom!

So, as I worked in the yard, and journaled in the evenings, I spent many hours pondering the meaning of the dream with the stairs. In my dream, my arms were outstretched above my head as I reached the top of the stairs, and I was filled with a great joy. *Where was that joy now? I certainly had not felt it in my marriage for these many years, and I did not feel it now.* I did understand that the male figure leaning on me as I climbed the stairs was Mark, representing how he had leaned on me emotionally through our many, many years of marriage. My search became, *Where was the joy? Did it mean there was another person, or another situation or circumstance that would bring me this great joy?*

Was it Jerry?

It was impressed upon me that the dream and vision of the cord snapping, went hand in hand.

As the cord snapped, I felt a strong sense that I had reached the top of the stairs, because *I could no longer be suppressed. I was caving in. I could no longer walk the stairs with the heavy weight on me. The difficult journey was over.*

The understandings made sense to my intellect, but I still could not feel the joy. It, quite simply, eluded me. I had to find it. I had already spent too many years without it. So my quest continued. And so did the nightmares and dreams.

The themes were similar, floods, fires, car accidents, snakes, rats, anything catastrophic or scary, and none of them left me feeling warm and fuzzy, and certainly not joyful. With each one, I carefully looked up the symbolism, still trying to add new insight to my hazy view.

One such nightmare was especially intense. I saw myself in a house, and it was burning. It seemed to only burn partially, and I put it out. But then I went back into the dream and the house burned more extensively. I ran through the house, and grabbed Kayla. Then, Mark, Kayla and I went outside. Erin apparently was at a school event, and we were going to meet her, because I went back inside the house to get tickets. When I went in, I had to climb a ladder to get into the garage. When I got to the top of the ladder, a large snake struck at me and bit me on the cheek. It was then that I woke up. According to *The Dream Book* by Betty Bethards, a house represents the self, and snakes are connected to our awakening. Fire is tied to cleansing, allowing the self to be open to higher knowledge.

One thing I knew for sure, everything was happening at a very deep level, and evolving so rapidly I could barely keep up.

As I continued journaling, I wrote not only my entries, but responses as I felt them coming to me. Here is one such entry:

> *Dear Carrie:*
>
> *I am walking with you now, as always. You need not be afraid if you continue stepping in small steps, one at a time. Continue to work on your own growth, and within your own sphere of influence, as you have. If you will continue setting your life in order, I will give you just enough to respond to, without it being overwhelming. I have New Horizons awaiting you. Do not fear the unknown. I am there to lead you through the haze, out into the light . . .*
>
> *Love,*
> *Your Heavenly Father*

This leads me to the second dilemma I was encountering. *What would I do?* There were no clear answers. I struggled, begged, and pleaded for an answer that I could cling to. It did not come. What I did realize was that I needed to study it in my mind to discover my path. By using my reasoning abilities, I could make my own choice. I felt there was not a right choice. God was leaving it up to me, his love is so great. After all, he did give us our agency, right? The only thing I could do was to trust in the thoughts that were taking residence within me. It was so difficult when I had not been doing that throughout my life. I was a stranger to myself. I rehearsed that "I was a wonderful, beautiful person with much to offer. I deserved happiness."

It was the spring of 1996.

The dresser was almost finished. I sat in the side yard soaking up the warm sunshine as I worked to re-finish the wood so that it was restored to new. Change hung in the air, and I was preparing for it. I started using Formby's finish, advertised as "the easy way." As I worked to remove the old finish and clean off the old stains, I realized, *there really is no easy way.* I thought how much that was true of relationships. *If the old crusty layers underneath aren't removed completely, the shiny, smoother surface can't show through on top. The delicate wood patterns will not be enhanced. It struck me that it takes a great deal of effort and time, but that it is well worth the end result. Each task builds on a previous task. One must be completed thoroughly and completely in order to move on to the next. Steps cannot be skipped or rushed in order to enjoy the full benefit.*

The joy comes in knowing you've given fully and completely to the task, and can then enjoy the outcome of sharing it's beauty and utility over time. It struck me that unless the foundation is secure, nothing else looks right or falls into place. With the right combination, the natural beauty of the wood will radiate. If not, it becomes buried and perhaps even lost. My marriage felt like the bottom crusty layers. I could see how we would need to start over to re-build the layers to create a beautiful finish. We needed to start back at the foundation.

Finally, I had the insight I needed to move forward. I knew that there could be no marriage with Mark unless we started over completely.

I felt that we would have to build a new foundation. The only way I thought this could be done, was to separate and then take steps back in that direction. I needed to be away and get my head cleared.

So the girls and I moved into an apartment in Vacaville, California. It was just in time for Kayla to start kindergarten.

It was September, 1996.

Erin would be starting middle school, and we would be living in the attendance area. No more commuting over the hills from Fairfield. Mark stayed in the house, begrudgingly. He said that we would never get back together now, because I had left him.

I didn't know any other way.

> *Dear Carrie:*
>
> *The path is already set before you, if you will take one step at a time. My hand is there for you to take, so I can walk along with you. Give me your fear, you no longer need to carry it. I am always with you, even when you are not aware of it. I am with you now, and if you will continue to seek me, you will feel that clarity that you desire to make choices that you will feel good about.*
>
> *Love,*
> *Your Heavenly Father*

I marveled that even in this circumstance, I still felt God's loving presence with me.

The path where we were heading became apparent.

CHAPTER 18

INNER JOURNEY

We were at Sally and Jim's for our regular couple's get together. We were watching videos from the marriage and family series "The Five Love Languages," by Dr. Gary Chapman. Our friends Tina and Garrett were part of the group, as well as other friends from our church family. We enjoyed lots of fun interactions and kidding around.

"So Carrie, what Myer's Briggs personality type are you?" Sally inquired.

"I'm an INFJ, I answered, what about you?" I tossed back.

"Well, I'm close to you. I'm an INTJ," Sally shared.

"Hey, me too," threw in Tina.

Since Jim was a Marriage and Family Therapist, he always had interesting activities that he added to our time together. We had just taken the Myers-Briggs Type Indicator, which is a personality inventory assessment, helpful in understanding differences in temperament and styles of interaction. Each of the sixteen patterns predict a specific way of interacting with the world.

The first letter can be either "I" or "E," correlating to introvert or extrovert tendencies. The second letter, "N" or "S," means intuitive, or subjective, suggesting that an individual is guided more by hunches, or experience. The third letter refers to "T" or "F," meaning that the individual primarily interacts through their thought processes, or feelings. Lastly, "P" and "J," imply that an individual is more inclined towards planning or being more spontaneous. These are simplified explanations for a much more detailed theory.

Mark interjected that he was an ESTP, my opposite.

"That's OK, Sally and I are as good as opposites too. I'm an ESTP as well," said Jim.

Garrett replied, "Tina and I are the same, INTJ."

I thought about my parents since I'd shared the inventory with them. Mom was ENFJ, and Dad, ISTJ. Interesting, I thought, they are nearly opposites as well. Maybe that's why I took the role of peacemaker in the family, I laughed.

The sound of the BART train outside the apartment window thrust me back to reality.

That was back in 1990, years before. *I guess there's no easy solution to relationships that work, I thought. Sally and Jim are opposites and they're still together.*

In fact, Sally and Jim continued to support me whether married, or separated. They were true friends. Sally had brought over a chair to help fill my living room with furniture. When I told her about my distress with not having enough money to buy food, she gave me $100. My meager salary of $24,000 was being stretched thin, living on my own with Erin and Kayla.

It was getting late and I needed to gather my wits so that I could get to my counseling appointment while Erin and Kayla were at swimming practice. They'd both been on the neighborhood swim team since Kayla turned three. It had become a summer ritual to spend mornings at practices. It was also the only time I had to squeeze in appointments when the girls were occupied.

As I drove, I thought about how much I liked the new therapist. Dr. Lewis had been great, but my Kaiser sessions had run out since there was a limited allotment under my coverage. Thank goodness Mark was continuing to cover our health insurance. I don't know what I would have done without it. Technically, we were not together, but I hesitated to file for divorce until I felt more resolved. Since the girls and I moved out, we only saw Mark when he stopped by.

Dr. Stewart was waiting when I arrived, as usual. I seemed to always be running five minutes behind. I would have to work on that. She asked what had been going on for me since our last meeting.

"I've been thinking a lot about marriage and what my responsibility in the relationship has been," I responded.

"What do you think about that?" she chirped.

There she goes again, always throwing it back on me, I diverted.

"Mark has really done a lot of things in my direction in the past few years. He got a vasectomy, without my request. He's bought me gifts, taken me on a dinner and dance cruise, set up a Valentine's Day scavenger hunt, and even learned to do woodworking so he could build me a bookshelf. He said he would re-marry me if I wanted," I stated.

"And?" she encouraged me on.

"Well, it didn't change my feelings, and since the girls and I moved out, he hasn't done anything in my direction. He came over the other day, leaned over to kiss me, and said, "Nope, don't feel anything.""

"That must be confusing," she clarified.

"Yes, it really is, and it doesn't make me think he's been sincere," I added. "I am having a hard time trusting him and believing in what he says because his actions aren't consistent. I still have years of pain from not being treated very well that I have to figure out how to erase. I'm having a hard time moving past that," I moaned.

"That's understandable," she commented, "Does Mark listen to your feelings about your pain?"

"That's just it," I chided, "He wants me to move forward with him, and just forget it, at least he wanted me to move forward with him. Now he doesn't say that."

"What does he say?" she queried.

"Well, just what I said, that he doesn't feel anything for me. He has no patience for hearing about the past," I relayed.

"So, Carrie, let's get back to the original question, what is your responsibility in the marriage?"

"Oops, I guess I got side-tracked again," I said.

"It's always easier to see the other person as being at fault, but that's not your purpose in being here today, is it?" she continued.

"No, I guess not," I agreed.

She sat and waited for me to respond. I collected my thoughts.

"I know that being so attached to Jerry did not help us. I wanted Mark to look as bad as possible and make everything his fault so I'd alleviate my guilt at wanting to be with Jerry. I know it left holes in me where it might have been parts of myself I could have given to Mark and our marriage. I know I've needed to let go completely of Jerry before I could return to Mark," I introspected.

"Do you think you have been able to do that?" she questioned.

"Yes, I think so, but I still very much want the love and acceptance I felt from Jerry, in my marriage. I'm not willing to let that go," I stated energetically.

"I know I've been paying him back these past few years, for all the pain he caused me for the first fourteen years. I haven't kept myself up, thinking that I wanted Mark to prove his acceptance of me, no matter what. I've been looking for what was wrong with him, instead of what was right. I pushed him away and denied his needs many times, because of his offensive approach. I think I could have looked beyond that to what he was really saying," I pondered.

"Would you want to continue your relationship?" she asked, curiously.

"I can let go of the anger and pain now, and feel some love for him. I think I could be in the marriage the way I need to be now. I think I could extend myself now in ways I haven't been able to in the past. We did have pockets of time where we shared some pretty good sex. I think it was when I was able to open up more, and be more awake to my needs and desires. I think it's just hard to express them sometimes," I mused.

"Carrie, have you ever really had a marriage?" she probed.

She caught me totally off guard.

"What do you mean?" I pushed back.

"If marriage is a joining of two persons, have you ever really been together?" she explained.

"I guess not. No, you're right, we've always been at odds. I am having a hard time totally letting go because I don't want to hurt the girls. It is already becoming difficult for them. I'm afraid of what's ahead for them. I just think that he and I have had a hard time being emotionally intimate. We've needed to be more vulnerable and open. We needed to just have more fun together. We've both used wedges to keep the other person at a distance instead of moving closer together. I wonder, could we create more of a marriage now?"

"Could you?" she edged me on.

"Not when Mark is unwilling to make different choices. I think he's been engaging in sex talk on-line, and I don't want the same rejection and lack of respect I have had for the past seventeen years. He expresses no desire to come my way. I think he likes being on his own, less responsibility for sure," I quipped.

"Well, our time is up for today," she interjected. "Guess I'll see you next week?"

"OK," I replied.

I wonder what would be in store for me next time we got together.

CHAPTER 19

THE JOURNEY CONTINUES

There were some understandings that I came to.

First of all, perhaps the great joy I felt in the dream was just me, by myself, learning to love myself, being alive to myself and to life, and to my path and purpose, and that it was NOT any particular person or circumstance that would create my happiness. The joy at the top was in feeling love, acceptance, and freedom. Freedom to be myself. Freedom from the weights that I felt for so long. The agony of the climb was of my repressed self, because I so badly didn't want conflict or separation in my marriage, and because of my experience of marriage.

It became very clear that Mark had no intention of reconciling. The patterns of behavior were the same, only in a new environment.

I was learning to trust. Trust in the future. Trust in others. Trust in myself. I was learning to trust in what I was feeling and the thoughts that were coming to me, guiding me, and moving me forward. I was learning to trust in the fact that I am a wonderful and beautiful creation of God, that has much to offer. I was learning to trust that I could do things I had never done before, and that I could be in new situations and be able to deal with them.

I attended a workshop presented by Patricia Evans, author of the book, *The Verbally Abusive Relationship*." I began to see myself with a new perspective. I needed to be able to recognize my feelings and express them. I learned it was OK to feel whatever I felt. From the Catholic Retrouvaille program, I learned that we had engaged in unhealthy interactions, including blaming. In Patricia Evan's workshop I understood even more about the crazy making that had been in our marriage. I understood why I felt discounted, because I was.

I got more in touch with my feelings of inadequacy.

This was on my mind as I was driving to my counseling appointment. "*Good, I'm on time this week,*" I congratulated myself.

Dr. Stewart greeted me with, "How did the week go?"

"I did a lot of thinking about what you said," I replied.

"Oh yea, what did I say?" she shot back. *There she goes again*, I thought.

"What you said about not really being married," I responded.

"What did you think about it?" she shot back again.

"It made me think about marriage in a deeper way, that marriage is about what is happening between people," I relayed.

"Uh-huh," she nodded.

There was uneasy silence. I never knew what to say when it got quiet. Well, I guess I'll just keep talking about what's on my mind, I thought.

"I went to a workshop last weekend, that Patricia Evans did," I shared.

"What was it about?" she queried.

"Verbally abusive relationships," I responded.

"Do you think you were in a verbally abusive relationship?" she asked.

"I never thought about it that way, but maybe so," I suggested.

"What did you learn at the workshop?" she questioned further.

"That I must feel very inadequate to have been part of this for so many years," I stated.

"Where in your upbringing did you feel inadequate that may have affected who you were in your marriage?" she probed.

"I always felt inadequate as a woman because of my small breasts," I responded, "I'm not sure where I got it, but my dad and brother must have made remarks about women's breasts. I remember Gina, my sister, being larger than me. It seemed like she got more attention that way."

"Why do you look so sad right now?" she poked.

"I was just thinking about something that happened with my neighbor, while he babysat us," I said softly.

"Would you like to tell me about it?" she asked.

"When I was about eleven, he was running around the house naked and forced himself on top of my sister and me. I remember being really scared," I relayed, embarrassingly.

"That must have affected you a lot," she summarized.

"Yea, I guess so," I mumbled.

"Carrie, you were molested," she stated emphatically.

"Oh, really?" I replied, "he had an erection, but he didn't put it inside me, he just poked."

"Yes, Carrie, that's molestation," she stated again.

Why does she keep pushing this so hard? She's talking about my neighbor. He was fifteen years old and didn't really know better. He was just being hormonal, I thought, in his defense.

"The reason I'm pushing this with you is because I think it's important information that may have affected intimacy in your marriage," she continued.

I never thought about that, in fact it had been years since I even remembered the incident.

"Were there other incidents where you were advanced sexually when you were growing up?" she probed.

"Sure, lots of 'em." I retorted.

"Like?" she pressed.

"The time I was sixteen years old and I was at camp. I was putting together the camp yearbook and needed to go into town to use the copy machine at the church. The director of the camp took me in his car, and when we got inside, he cornered me in the copy room and leaned in to try and kiss me," I shared.

"Did he kiss you?" she inquired.

"No, I turned my head, but it made me very uncomfortable."

"What else?" she pressed.

"The time I was sixteen and babysitting for an eleven year old. He was super strong and literally pulled me up the stairs and tried to get me in his parents' bedroom and implied that he would try to have his way with me." I grappled for the right words to use.

"Did he have his way with you?" she pressed on.

"No, but my arms ached and ached for days from fighting him so hard, and I never babysat for him again," I confessed.

"You never told anyone about these incidents?" she investigated.

"No, none of them," I replied.

"That's a lot for one person to experience," she observed.

"There were lots of other events too. After I was married, I walked across the bridge at our church campgrounds, and another married man walked up beside me and tried to clasp hands with me, you know, locking fingers in an intimate way. Another time, when I lived on my own in an apartment, someone tried to pry the door open, because my roommate and I saw big chunks of wood carved out from around the lock." *I was beginning to realize that she was right. There was a lot I had gone through that involved others crossing physical boundaries with me.*

"How do you think it has affected your marriage?" she pressed.

"I guess it goes back to the trust issue. It was hard to trust Mark, that he had good intentions. It seemed like he set about proving that he wasn't trustworthy by the behaviors he engaged in that made it even harder to get close," I suggested.

"What is it about you that has attracted all these experiences?" she teased, like a carrot dangling in front of me.

"I guess because I was always really shy and non-assertive. Maybe other people have gotten the idea they could get away with it," I painfully relayed.

"Do you think that is true of you now?" she picked further.

"No, I feel a lot stronger and I'm not nearly so shy. I think quiet would be a better word to describe me," I said.

"So, let's talk about anger," she proposed, "a couple of weeks ago you mentioned that it has been hard for you to deal with."

"Yes, especially with people close to me. Lately Erin's been angry a lot. When that happens, I freeze. It's like I become helpless and can't deal with it. It almost feels like I am back in the marriage and being verbally attacked," I heave.

"When it happens, Carrie, just try to stay in the moment and keep breathing," she suggested.

That's exactly what I needed to do. Stay in the moment and keep breathing.

"Well, time's up until next week," she sighed, "keep practicing staying in the moment and see how it goes."

I need to remember that, I repeated, just stay in the moment and keep breathing.

CHAPTER 20

LOOKING BACK

We divorced in October, 1997.

In a vow to myself, I did not step outside my apartment door to engage in any other relationship, for a full six months. During that time, Mark and I each wrestled with ourselves, exchanged a few letters, and tried to maintain what was best for the girls. My journaling continued, as I reflected on my life in its new form. The more time passed, the more I realized that the new transformation that I fantasized about, was not going to take place for us. I grew into a place of acceptance. Acceptance of what was, and what might be. *Would I be alone now, with no companionship, outside of the girls?*

I started to think that it would be better than what we had. As long as I knew that I could be honored and cherished elsewhere, I could not go back where that did not happen. I also had grown to see that perhaps this would also be better for the girls. Erin had started developing such anxiety when we were together the last few years, that she had actually licked sores into her little chin.

I felt horrible.

In my counseling sessions, I continued to spend time examining what my part in the relationship had been. What did I need to own, and change? Certainly the energy I sent Jerry's way, didn't help. But I knew there was much more to it than that. I was re-awakening to myself.

I became intensely aware of the energy all around me. After getting on the other side of my anger and grief, I felt vibrant and alive in ways that had been long forgotten. I began to experience the joy that I foresaw in my dream. I felt the beauty within and around me like never before.

I learned that I had choices, and that I had always had them. I didn't want to let go of these new feelings I was experiencing. I was learning to give myself value and not rely on seeking that in outside relationships. I was worthy of joy. I knew that Mark had continued making choices sexually, that devalued me. Sure, he had seen a counselor, but didn't think he had issues in this area. I had decided I wasn't willing to live with behaviors that made me feel worthless.

As I examined our relationship I could see how I blamed him when there were problems. I could have focused more on his strengths, instead of his weaknesses. I could have tried harder to let go of the past, and open myself up to the present. I could have been more forgiving. I could have taken better care of myself, and become more independent. *Would all of these things have made a difference?*

We had, after all, chosen our paths. We each had difficulty with being intimate, in our own ways. We had developed habits of relating in unhealthy ways to try and get our needs met. Even when we turned those around, there was not the connection that we needed in order to create a marriage. In spite of it all, I had kept trying.

Someone once shared with me their definition of perfection as, "being the best you can be in any given moment." Thinking of that definition has helped elevate me to forgiveness, for Mark, and for myself. I was, indeed, responding as best I could all along the way. Who's to say that Mark wasn't doing the same? I was not walking in his shoes. *Whenever any of us are drawing from a well with no reserve, we will come up short.*

Looking back, I know I had signs that I could have heeded, that told me marrying Mark was probably not the best path for me to take. I ignored them. I like the saying from Maya Angelou where she says, *When someone shows you who they are, believe them the first time.* I should have read her books years ago. However, I wouldn't have the beautiful children I have, and I wouldn't have learned so many life lessons.

Following divorce proceedings in February 1997, I stepped out into the world as a single parent, in March of that same year. Never in my wildest dreams would I have imagined the friendship that awaited me.

The girls were not accustomed to having a sitter, so I tried to make it as painless as possible.

"There's pizza in the refrigerator," I hollered, as I stepped outside to get into my car.

"Yea," they cheered in unison, "When will you be back?" they asked almost as quickly.

"You'll probably be asleep when I return. It'll be OK, Jennifer is lots of fun. She'll play games with you," I explained.

"We don't want you to go, Mom," they both complained.

I picked up the pace so they didn't have time to convince me to stay. *Why did I feel guilty?*

Didn't I deserve to have time for myself to have fun? I guess this is something to bring up at the next counseling session, I reflected.

I was all dressed up in a black lace, long-sleeved evening dress and high heels. I wasn't accustomed to wearing heels, so it felt a little out of my element as I climbed the stairs leading away from the apartment entrance. I had only worn the dress on one other occasion. It just seemed like dressing up was the thing to do to get in a celebratory mood. I breathed in the smell of eucalyptus and pine hovering over the complex. I was also breathing in a new beginning.

Now that I was in my car driving away, *where was I going to go? I had no idea.* I was alone.

What about a movie? No, not by myself. What about going dancing? I wouldn't know where to go. In college, I had gone to every dance that had been held. I loved it! However, that wasn't something we did when I was married, unless it was a special function. *I know*, I thought, *I'll go sing karaoke.* I remembered what Dr. Lewis said, "You need to sing," is what she'd said. That would be fun! It had been a long time since I'd done that.

The only place I could think of that had karaoke that I knew of, was Benihana's. It was actually a fancy Japanese restaurant not too far away. They had a lounge area just inside the entrance to the restaurant where I had seen a karaoke set-up. I started heading that way.

Waves of discomfort settled over me as I stepped inside the bar. I was never comfortable in bars. I didn't drink. That's ridiculous, I told myself, you're not going to be drinking. You came here to sing. Just get a glass of water or juice. As I considered these ideas, I glanced around the room to figure out where I would sit. I spotted a plush sofa where there was another female sitting alone. I decided to go sit across from her.

She acknowledged my presence, but didn't say too much. We exchanged names. I found out her name was Diana.

"What brings you here, Diana?" I questioned.

"I am waiting to meet up with someone I met while chatting on-line," Diana explained.

I joked, "Maybe it is my ex-husband."

At that suggestion, she turned a little white and apologetically stated, "I hope not."

She continued with, "In fact, I have been waiting here for some time and if he doesn't show up in the next fifteen minutes, I'm out of here."

"Where will you go?" I wondered.

"I don't know, is there any place you want to go?" she invited.

"Well, I really wanted to go dancing, but I didn't know where to go," I clarified.

"I know a great place to go dancing, out in Vallejo, so if he doesn't show up, let's go together. What do you say?" she prodded.

"Sounds great to me," I replied.

"So, you didn't say what you are doing here, Carrie," she tentatively asked.

"Today is the first day out my door since separating from my husband six months ago. We are in the process of divorcing and I didn't think I could stand one more day to not go out and do something socially. I guess it's also a kind of celebration for my new life." I laid all my cards on the table for her consideration.

"Oh, I'm sorry," she empathized, "do you mind my asking how you ended up being divorced?"

"No, it's OK, basically, he didn't treat me very nicely," I explained. *That seemed like the easiest explanation, even though I knew it was a lot more complicated than that.*

"I've been there," she continued empathizing, "know what I say to guys now? I tell 'em to get on the nearest bus, 'cause there's a whole lot more guys where they came from, and they're not worth my time if they don't treat me right."

I laughed. *I like her way of thinking. This could be good for me.* I examined Diana more closely. She had short, dark hair that was neatly curled under at the shoulder. She was filled out in an attractive, full-figured way. What I liked best was the easy-going way about her. She laughed robustly, and her eyes sparkled in a fun-loving sort of way. *I wish I could be more like her*, I thought.

We shared a few more laughs before she announced that she was leaving. "No more waiting for me," she stated emphatically, "he had his chance."

With that announcement, she signaled for me to follow her out to where we were parked. So much for karaoke, but I was excited about going dancing and was curious to see what the dance hall would be like.

We followed each other to Vallejo so that each of us would be free to leave when we were ready to go. I quickly sized up where we were headed. It looked like a combination restaurant and bar. I could hear the loud rock music in the parking lot before we ever went inside.

The parking lot was jammed so it was tough finding a spot.

We found a table and joined two others who were already sitting there. *What would my mother say? I had already talked to strangers twice tonight.*

Conversation was difficult over the loud music, but I found that I didn't have much time for talking anyway, because I was only there a very short time when I was approached by dance partners. *Most of them were much younger than me.*

We danced and laughed until I was exhausted. I knew it was time to head home, otherwise I wouldn't be able to stay awake. Dan had been the dance partner that clung most tightly to me, and was the last man standing, so to speak, at the end of the evening. He walked me to my car.

Then he pointed out his car. *There was a bright blue Cadillac. Was I worthy of being with someone like this?*

"Could I have your phone number?" Dan hinted, "I'd like to see you again."

"Sure, I'll write it down for you," I offered.

After giving Dan my phone number, Diana and I reflected on the evening's events.

"Can you believe that, Carrie, in one evening you snagged a looker?" she exclaimed enthusiastically.

"I'm a little amazed, I must admit, I never expected to have anything like this happen to me," I confessed.

"See, you have to believe in yourself. You're an attractive woman. Let's do this again sometime," Diana suggested.

"Sounds like fun, let's get each other's phone numbers," I said.

As she pulled away, I thought, *maybe being single isn't going to be so bad after all.*

Thank you, God, for watching out for me.

CHAPTER 21

SOULMATES

Dear Carrie:

The path is already set before you, if you will take one step at a time. My hand is there for you to take, so I can walk along with you. Give me your fear, you no longer need to carry it. I am always with you, even when you are not aware of it. I am with you now, and if you will continue to seek me, you will feel that clarity that you desire to make choices that you will feel good about.

As you feel led, respond to one thought, impression, or insight at a time. That will lead to further thoughts and impressions. As you seek me, and respond, the clouds will gradually fade away. I can make your life much easier. Give your stress and burdens to me. I long to take them from you. I can grant you hope and a clearer, brighter vision of the future. Go now, lighter and freer, knowing that I am with you.

Love,
Your Heavenly Father

Dan called the following Wednesday, while we were washing dishes from dinner.

"Carrie?" he inquired, "Is that you?"

"Yes," I hesitated. *Did I know this person?*

"It's Dan, remember we met last weekend?" he explained

"Oh yes, sorry, you caught me off guard," I rationalized.

"I wondered if you'd like to go to church with me. Have you ever been to Unity Church?" he inquired.

"No, but I've heard good things about it. I think I know where it is."

"They have great meditation. I love it. Want to meet there, say, 10:00 a.m.?

"Perfect, I'll see you then," I chimed in, as I hung up the phone. *Dan, he's the cute guy.* My mind wandered back to Saturday night when we'd danced the night away, with my new friend Diana. Dan was tall, probably about six feet tall. Mark was five feet eight inches, much shorter than Dan. I wasn't used to the height. Dan impressed me, with his sport coat and neatly styled shoulder-length hair. He moved smoothly on the dance floor too, something I admired. *Now I find out he enjoys meditation. Unbelievable! What other surprises were in store for me?*

Sunday came quickly. I looked forward to our meeting with great anticipation, and nervousness. This was all so new to me. I reminisced about my dating years in college. I was a little rusty, and much older! I definitely needed a tune-up in the dating department! I decided to just keep breathing, and take it in stride. What else could I do?

When I met Dan outside the church building, he didn't disappoint me. He was every bit as attractive as I remembered him to be. He proved himself to be very polite as well. He opened the door as we stepped inside. People at the church were very friendly and embracing. I liked that.

The service was challenging and inspiring. The meditation was as engaging as Dan said. I enjoyed the visit so much that I would go back many more times over the next few years. It would become a healing refuge for me.

Afterwards, we went outside to the patio. I soon discovered that this was the "visiting place," where everyone mingled. Dan introduced me to so many people that my head was spinning with names. I doubted that I would be able to remember them all.

However, one name stuck with me. Her name was Katie. I immediately felt a connection with her. Dan introduced her as his "sister," although they were both chuckling about it, so I figured that didn't mean they were blood relatives. She said they had been friends for a long time and that they were both from Michigan. When Dan was occupied elsewhere, she pulled me aside and said, "Be careful. I like you and don't want to see you get hurt. Dan's had lots of girlfriends, but none of them for very long." I thanked her, at the same time not knowing how much I could trust her to tell me the truth. *She must be interested in him, I decided.*

After church, Dan suggested that we go walking at the nearby park. It was nice weather and Erin and Kayla were at their dad's for the weekend, so I said, "Sure."

That week Dan called me again and invited me to a single's dance that was being held near where I lived. He called it a St. Patrick's Day Dance, so I should wear green. I would have to do some scrambling to find something green. I didn't usually wear that color. Also, I would have to get another babysitter for Erin and Kayla. I hated that, but didn't want to turn down this opportunity, so I said, "yes, I would go."

Dan picked me up in his Jaguar. *What? He had two nice cars?* I was stunned. Turns out he was an engineer so he made a pretty substantial income. That in combination with not having his own family, made for a pretty lucrative lifestyle.

"Hi Carrie," I heard from behind me. I turned to see that it was Katie. I felt jealousy start to creep in. *Don't do that Carrie, you're being silly. You don't even know if they are interested in being together.* Over the course of the evening I observed their interactions and saw that they were very close. I also noticed that Katie hugged others and acted just as close. *That must be the way she is,* I noted.

We sat at the same table together with Katie and I found out that she had two daughters too.

Hers were older, but I was grateful to meet someone that perhaps could understand what I was going through as a single parent with girls. She told me stories of living in her own house and being very involved in her girls' activities. She also conveyed a very positive outlook on life and was very complimentary and encouraging of me. I began to see why Dan liked her so much. She expressed a desire to be friends and I returned her interest. I wanted to get to know her better.

Dan and I spent many dates together over the next nine or ten months. He introduced me to the single's world as he took me to many dances, sponsored by different organizations. We shared many Unity activities, and we took lots of hikes. He introduced me to lots of other singles. We watched movies at his condo. He even invited me to go to his sister's (real sister) house for Christmas. Then one day he just stopped calling with no explanation.

"Katie I need to talk to you," I gushed.

"What's going on," she probed from her end of the line.

"Dan's not calling me. Do you know what is happening?" I wondered.

"Carrie, you're giving him too much. Remember when I warned you when you'd first met?"

Guys want to be the hunters and be given a challenge. You're making it too easy and maybe he's grown disinterested," she explained.

I had learned a lot about Katie, including knowing that she wouldn't hurt a flea. The words stung just the same, because she had become a good friend, she was giving me the truth. "How am I giving him too much?" I inquired.

"Carrie, you're always baking things for him, and you're always available. When's the last time you told him "no" when he asked you to go somewhere with him?"

"You're right. I see that now, but it still hurts, Katie."

"I'm sorry Carrie. I was afraid this would happen. He preys on newly divorced, vulnerable women, then moves on to someone new."

"I guess I don't want to have someone like that it my life anyway," I mulled.

"Now you're talking. You're a drop dead beautiful woman. Any guy would be lucky to be with you," *that was Katie, always the flatterer. I so appreciated her.* I needed building up, and lots of it, so I soaked it up like a sponge. Katie had come into my life just when I needed her.

"So Carrie, when are you going to start looking at houses?" Katie poked. She had been trying to get me to consider it for months now. I had complained to her that it was getting tough with the three of us cooped up in an apartment.

"I know you can do it, Carrie. If I can do it, you can do it. Anything is possible if you only believe. Keep focusing on the possibilities and you will be amazed," were Katie's encouraging words. *Always the optimist, that's Katie.*

Thank you, Katie. Thank you, God, for her friendship.

CHAPTER 22

BITTERSWEET EMBRACE

It was summer 1998.

We found ourselves once again in Santa Cruz for family camp. The air was thick with memories. Memories that included our family when it was whole. Memories of Erin and Kayla when they were young, and innocent, and more protected from the pain in the world. The pain of divorce and the pain of being in a small apartment with very few things. Not that it was all bad, but I hurt for them and the losses they were feeling. The losses I was feeling had taken their toll as well.

Being in Santa Cruz took us away from those realities, temporarily. We could bask in the love and friendship of people we'd known for many years, here at family camp. Erin was now twelve years old, and Kayla had just turned seven. Both of them loved being here with friends that had become special to them. They could feel the acceptance and nurturing of the adults that had become like family to us.

Erin was baptized in the swimming pool when she was eight years old. Vivid memories of a dove swooping down over the pool just as the prayer was said, flooded my mind as I reflected back. Another time I was eating in the dining hall, and turned around to see Erin standing naked behind me. She was about five or six years old at the time. I shrieked for her to immediately go back to the cabin and put her clothes on. I watched to make sure that she followed my directions, and saw a line of little boys trailing behind her. Erin always knew how to get attention, even though in that instance I don't think it was intentional.

Erin and Kayla interrupted my thoughts as they ran up, smiling in wide purple-stained grins. In was easy to tell where they'd been. They found great pleasure in picking raspberries that clung to the thick vines hanging along the fence that ran the length of the backside of the pool, along the creek's edge. At any given moment, they could be spotted there, which made it easy to keep track of where they were.

The other attraction for the girls was the tire swing. It hung from a monumental redwood tree with a truck tire dangling from a long, thick rope that invited fully extended swoops of delight from its occupants. If they were not on the swing, they were waiting their turn in line, or were at the raspberry thicket.

The camp schedule was laid out so that adults had classes together in the mornings, while the children attended their own meetings. Morning worships started our day, following by sessions that launched passionate discussions about the topics being presented. In the Mission of Christ Church we were allowed a wide range of our own interpretations, because we each have our own relationship with God. We therefore can discern our own truth.

In the afternoons, we recreated. The little valley was encircled by hills that made it a cozy hide-away. The cool, sometimes foggy mornings, gave way to warm, soothing sunshine. This was my favorite time. I enjoyed sitting in the sun, reading or doing needlepoint. It was one of the few times during the year I felt I had that luxury. I wish it could be this way all the time, if only there were a way to capture this serene feeling and take it home with me.

I tried. I journaled and prayed as I always had, but being a single parent had made it more difficult. I'd always done the chores and cooking, but now all the decisions fell on my shoulders and at times was hard to bear. At least Mark had cooked breakfast on Saturday mornings. Those little things seemed like big things, now that I was carrying everything alone.

It would be so much easier if there was someone to share it with, and to help me, I reflected. I found that it was not easy maneuvering the landscape of singlehood. I was not only single, but I was a single parent. The girls were of primary importance, so I was learning to set up dates, for the most part, when they were with Mark. Then I could spend as much time as possible with them.

Now that they were becoming older, it seemed they needed me more than ever. It was hard for me to stay present, as Dr. Stewart suggested, when I dealt with so much internally.

My mind shifted back to the first fall we spent in the apartment. It was Thanksgiving.

"I want to take the girls to my parents for Thanksgiving," Mark stated.

I hesitated before answering. *What was he saying? I would not be part of their Thanksgiving this year?* The reality of this awareness took root.

"Why?" I asked.

"I thought it would be good for them. My relatives are the only family they have in California," he thoughtfully continued.

"Well, alright, they will like that," I sputtered. Even though I knew he was right, the words were like daggers in my heart. They would not be with me. It would be the first holiday I'd ever spent without them. I wrestled with absorbing his words. What if I went with them? No, we were separated and that would not help them adjust. He was not inviting me, and I didn't want to be in a tense situation. *What was I going to do?* I couldn't afford to fly home. I would have to figure it out. I guess I will have a little time to myself.

As it turned out, I had met a new friend Catherine, who invited me to spend Thanksgiving with her family. I didn't really know her well, but she somehow sensed my need and extended the invitation. She had three daughters who spent the day making a video. They ran through the house giggling, squealing, and thoroughly enjoying themselves. I appreciated the invitation and the opportunity to join with their family in the celebration. It only made me miss my family all the more.

On the way home the tears came pouring out. If the tears were raindrops, a flood would have been declared, because they wouldn't stop. Driving along I could barely see through my obscured vision.

Then, I felt a great big spiritual hug wrap around me like I have never felt it before. Immediately I thought of my grandmother, the one who had the dream about her husband, my maternal grandmother.

Throughout the months of our early separation I kept in close touch with my family in Iowa. My mother had told me that Grandma was getting progressively more ill. She had osteoporosis and suffered frequent hip fractures. Now, however, she had skin cancer on top of that and at her ripe age of ninety-two, there was not much fight left in her.

After my experience with the book *Power Evangelism*, I decided that I would send my energy to her, long distance. That was the only way I felt I could be present with her. I also thought I could reach out to elderly who were in my close proximity. I felt when I did something for someone else, I indirectly did it for my grandmother. At least that's what I told myself, and it made me feel better about not being with her. I also sent letters to express myself, afraid that I would not ever get the opportunity otherwise.

I don't know if Grandma ever felt my energy, but I kept sending it. It became a nighttime ritual, and cathartic for me. I began to grieve the potential loss of her presence in my life.

The quilt she had made many years before, offered me comfort.

"Hi Mom, how's Grandma doing?" I hesitantly asked, fearing the worst.

"She's not doing so well. She has not been aware of her surroundings for at least a week now. They don't give her a lot longer to be with us," she reported.

An immediate sense of urgency grabbed my attention. *You need to go home and see her*, was impressed upon my mind.

"I'm going to come out there. Let me look into tickets and I'll get back to you," I suggested.

Mom didn't argue, which wasn't like her. Usually she would try to make sure that I could afford it. Both my parents had a sense of how dire my financial situation had become. Now she said nothing about it. Internally I worried, *how would I pay for it? I had no money in the bank.*

Then I realized that I did indeed have money, it's just that it was all in Mark's name. I decided to call him and ask for the money.

Surprisingly enough, he didn't put up much fight, I think because it was about my sick grandmother.

It was the week of November 8th. I knew I needed to get there fast. I felt strongly that I didn't have much time. Erin, Kayla and I flew out the morning of November 11th, and went straight to Grandmother's side. Even though she was unconscious, when I entered the room, she rose up at the waist, extended her hand, and tried to mouth words that were inaudible. This scared the girls so they decided to spend time in the waiting room. My mom, uncle, sister and I lingered in the room where grandmother rested.

While in the room, I practiced sending my energy her way, and felt it returned. I knew in this way, what her energy felt like. We talked in quiet voices, reminiscing about stories of Grandma in our lives. Within a few hours we were abruptly interrupted when Grandma raised at the waist again, extended her hand forward, as if talking to someone we could not see, and then fell backwards. Mom said to Uncle Don, "She was talking to Dad, I know it." I felt Grandmother's energy pass over me, and looked over her way. She had passed. I knew it. The others knew her life had just ended as well, as tears were flowing. I shared my experience of feeling her energy pass through, and the others became aware of it too.

Mother shared with me later that a few months back, when Grandma had been more alert, she had shared concerns for me and told her that she had nightmares about me. I never knew what those nightmares were, because I didn't speak directly to her when she was coherent, and Mom didn't tell me about them. She said she didn't want to burden me. I pondered whether the nightmares were about my reality and that she was either experiencing in dreams what I had gone through, or was going through. *I never realized we were so connected.*

It was through this experience that I was able to recognize her embrace at Thanksgiving.

CHAPTER 23

LETTERS TO GRANDMA

July 12, 1996

Dear Grandma,

I wanted you to know some things, so thought I would write. Mom says that you have been in a lot of pain, and that it has been difficult to do very many things. I'm sorry that you're having to suffer so much. It doesn't seem right that someone so loving and giving as yourself, should have to suffer so much. But I believe that your life has continued to be a witness of love and strength, as those within your influence have observed how you handle yourself so gracefully.

Grandma, I think you've probably suffered far more than most people I know. I, along with everyone else, would like to have you around for a long time to come, but I would not want you to have to continue suffering. I know that your suffering has gone beyond physical pain, with the loss of your sight, to not be able to do things you've always enjoyed.

I wanted you to know that you have had an important impact on my life. You have always offered a quiet, sustaining strength, through your presence. I've always felt your love and support. I know that I will always feel that with me. I know the girls feel that from you as well, which I perceive in the way that they talk about you. There have been many nights that Erin and Kayla have included you in their bedtime prayers. I wanted you to know that there have been many times that you have been in my thoughts and prayers as well. I've learned that I can "send" loving energy through prayer and focused concentration. I've done that for you many times. I don't know if you have felt it, on your end.

I have several special "older" friends. One of them is exceptional, her name is Janet and she's part of our congregation. Would you believe she used to be a school cook also? Whenever I interact with her, I think of you. When I help her in some way, I've thought that somehow, by my action here, that someone would be reaching out to you in a way that you needed, there.

Did Mom tell you that I've had a call to an elder? I just realized that I had not shared that with you, directly. I've not written frequently, but you've been very much a part of me, and always will be. I want you to get well and not hurt anymore, but I want mostly what is best for you.

Even though I'm not there with you, I know that you're getting support, especially from Mom, Uncle Don, and Uncle Ben. If I thought for any reason that you wanted, or needed me there, I would be there. If you feel at all that way, I hope you would say so. I would be honored to be there with you, even though I would be limited to a weekend because I'm teaching summer school until August 6th.

I've found in recent years that the values I was raised with have become more and more important to me, and I will continue to move my life more and more in line with putting less and less emphasis on materials things, and moving closer to those people and things that really matter.

Kayla and Erin are both blossoming. Kayla's got a reputation for being very gentle. Remember when she kissed the sore on your leg? She is always quick with not only kisses, but big hugs. She loves her preschool. They have a miniature horse named "Cinnamon," chickens, goats, flower and vegetable gardens, even a teepee! Kayla has lots of fun there. I'm glad, and it makes it easier to leave her when I go off to work. She's starting to read and write lots. It's so much fun to see her artwork. Of course, she usually wants to draw the Rugrats! Kayla is also rapidly developing her more dramatic side and showing more and more of her vibrant personality.

Erin got the class award for "most likely to become a teacher," funny, huh, since her mom is a teacher? She has been a tutor for other kids, and I was pleased when she told me that other kids were coming to her on the playground to help them problem-solve. Would you believe that she's starting middle school, and Kayla will be in kindergarten? Time sure passes all too quickly.

Erin has had many struggles in the last several years, but as she's overcome difficulties, she's really shining. She excels in her schoolwork, including clarinet, and she just sang a solo for "Dorothy" in the "Wizard of Oz" musical production at her school. She is on swim team, and is beginning to reap rewards in progress, from working hard the last couple of years. She is in a dance show this week, as the end of the year production. She has become a very refined, professional dancer!

The quilt you made is still a favorite, the girls always try and use it first, but I don't always let them use it exactly how and when they want to. I want to make sure it lasts for a long time. The girls know you made it, so it is special to them too, and they like how soft it is.

We will continue to remember you.

I love you,
Carrie

August 21, 1996

Dear Grandma,

I have thought often of writing since I received your letter. I really appreciate your thoughtfulness, especially since I know it isn't easy for you to write. You ARE worthy of the things I said. Your quiet ways speak much louder than you may realize.

I am sorry to hear that you are having to suffer so much. It sounds like the pain medication they are giving you is helping you to feel a little better. I am glad you have good people to take care of you. It sounds like you have lots of interesting neighbors as well.

Thank you for sharing Mom and Dad for a visit in July. It was great to have them at camp with us. It was also very helpful for me, so that I could continue to go to work in the daytime. I'm sure it wasn't easy for you to be without their company and help. I think it was a very good week for us. I know the girls enjoyed being with them also.

Erin has finished swim team and earned a gold medal, which means she improved her own times twenty-one times. She has worked really hard, and I think it has been very gratifying for her. She got registered for middle school the other day, and is feeling really grown up, even though she is still very petite. She and another girl at church are planning a service in September.

Kayla is excited about kindergarten as well. She is in the same class as her boyfriend (a boy she got attached to in her daycare, at the age of two), so she's in heaven. She also has only twenty-three kids in her class. That's relatively unheard of out here. I think Kayla may get the best educational opportunities now, since there was a new law that just passed meaning her first and second grade years will only have twenty kids in them. I have her signed up for a piano keyboard class, since that is what she wants to do. Over the past nine months, she has consistently wanted to learn to play the piano, over anything else, so she must really want it!

Mom says that you feel you may not have much longer on this earth. If that is the case, I will miss you. I know I speak for the rest of my family as well. You have been very present with the girls even though we haven't been able to be out your way often. Did Mom tell you that Kayla has been having lots of questions about death and angels? She is set on the idea that when we die, we again become babies. She told me that at a very early age, and I don't know where she heard it. She said God told her.

Will you visit us in spirit, if you can? Mark thought he felt his grandmother's presence after Erin was born. When I went to breast feed her at night, I felt a very strong presence over my shoulder every night for about a week. It was kind of scary, until I felt the assurance that the presence was there to look over her, and not to harm her. Mark liked to think that it was his grandmother. He also dreamed of her presence during his transplant surgery.

From Erin:

I will miss you a lot when you go to Heaven. You have been my only great-grandma and I will remember you and that, always. You have meant the most to me.

Love,
Erin (great-granddaughter)

From Kayla:
Dear Grandma:

I'm going to miss you very much from you dying. I love you very much.

Love,
Kayla (great-granddaughter)
OOOOOOOOOOOOOOOOOOOOOOOOOOOOOOOOOOOOOOOOOOOOOO
OOOOOOOOOOOOOOOOOOOOOOO
XXXXXXXXXXXXXXXXXXXXXXXXXXXXXXXXXXXXXXXX
XXXXXXXXXXXX
I love Grandma and my cousins Brad and Ryan and Justin and kitty cats and rainbow sherbet ice cream.

Love eternally, from us all,
Carrie

CHAPTER 24

COUPON QUEEN

How was I going to provide for the girls and me on my meager salary? I was worried. Never before had I needed to make money stretch so far. The hardest part was telling the girls "no" when I wanted to say "yes" to requests they made. They had grown to accept going to the Goodwill Store to put together outfits for Halloween. In fact, I think they had fun with it, because they could be creative. It's not that they were used to having a lot, but they weren't used to it being so tight.

I realized it came down to two things, increasing my income and minimizing my expenses. It suddenly hit me that I had not reported my classwork from the past several years, to the school district office. I was now back in the regular classroom and no longer a school counselor, since there were no full-time positions available. Why had I not done this before? *I guess it's because we always had two incomes and I never was this desperate before.* That's crazy, I could have had more income before!

After collecting the transcripts, I took them to the district office and found that I had moved across on the salary schedule for the following school year. Yea! Victory! Now I was getting somewhere! I rejoiced. I needed to think of more ways to get income. It was still not going to be enough, even with the child support I now received since the divorce.

The phone rang, interrupting my reflections.

"Hello?" I said.

"Mrs. Cunningham?" the voice on the other end of the line asked.

Oh no, not a salesman, I bemoaned.

"I would like to give you a survey to see if you qualify to participate in our latest research study," she explained.

"For what?" I jabbed.

"If you qualify it would take seventy-five minutes of your time and you would get $80 cash," she explained further.

Bingo, more money! Well, this seemed easy enough!

"OK, I'll do it," I came back firmly.

After a series of questions about cleaning products I use around the house, how many people are in my household, how often do I shop, and a myriad of other interrogations that I thought would go on forever, she replied, "You qualify, we can use you. Are you available on Thursday evening at 5:00 p.m.?"

Ugh, 5:00 p.m., that's when the girls would be here. Maybe they'd be alright for that amount of time on their own. Erin was getting older and more responsible.

"Yes, I can make it," I replied excitedly. Maybe I can share a special treat with the girls to elicit their support.

I looked at my watch. It was 6:00 p.m., and I had told Katie I would meet her at the Chinese restaurant so we could eat before the dance started at 8:00 p.m. We were spending more and more time together while the girls were at their dad's. Katie was not only a lot of fun, but she was very wise and readily consoled me as I shared with her the challenges I was going through. She understood too, because she'd raised her own daughters and had gone through a divorce herself.

"Can I have this dance?" came a voice from behind, echoing in my ear.

"Hi Bill," I beamed. Bill had become one of my regular dance partners. He learned that I could easily flow into the twists, turns and twirls he frequently instigated. I thoroughly enjoyed the feeling of having a man in control of my body's sway and rhythm. It was a feeling I could get used to. I had begun to enjoy getting dressed up too.

Sometimes I felt awkward though because I knew the mini-skirts and dolled-up hair were not me. I was more of a jean's gal. Give me a grassy meadow and I'll curl up and read a book or watch the stars and listen to the birds sing. Yes, maybe I would dance in the meadow too. But being dressed up put me on display as an object for male viewing. After all, they were shopping. Did they like the way I looked, or did they not? I was back in the meadow picking daisies.

I was shopping too. I liked to think that more was going into my selection than a random choice of daisy pedals. That's how it felt at these dances, however.

"John, great to see you," I chirped, as I again was whisked away into yet another man's arms. It was beginning to feel a lot like college where I'd spent a lot of time bouncing around between lots of different men. It wouldn't be long before someone else came along capturing my attention.

Whereas I had lots of dance partners, Katie took first prize. She not only captured the men's attention, she captured their hearts because she took such a personal interest in each one. I was still learning how to connect on more personal levels, in this new environment.

When it was time to go, we compared notes and found that we had each spent the entire evening on our feet, dancing non-stop. I felt like a pretty teenager again. *Who would have thought it would be like this for me?*

"There's a craft fair tomorrow, would you like to go?" Katie inquired.

"Sure, sounds like fun!" I exclaimed.

We each went directly home. This was getting to be a strain on my old, tired body, I thought.

It was getting tiring having interest from men because of what I looked like. I was anxious to connect with a man because he liked who I was. Sometimes I engaged in conversations with the men at the dances, but it was difficult to hear, and some of them were drinking a lot of alcohol and had a glassy-eyed look that made me wonder if anyone was home.

There must be a part of me that still needs all this attention, I thought, as I turned these ideas over in my head.

On Sunday, Katie and I met at the annual craft fair that was held at the fairgrounds. I had fun keeping my eye out for small decorations that would fit the country decor of my apartment, or things the girls would like. Katie would look for decorations for her house as well, and items her daughters or grandkids would like. It was a day well spent and there were always new items to capture our interest.

We passed a booth that didn't look like crafts. I approached the counter to see what it was.

"Carrie it's just a timeshare," Katie interjected.

"What do you mean?" I said.

"A timeshare, where you go and listen to a presentation and they try to sell it to you," reiterated Katie.

"Hi, we represent the Southwind Resorts. Are you available next week?" a young, eager man recited.

"Why?" I inquired.

"If you can attend one of our presentations we will give you a $100 Macy's gift card," he continued.

Wow, a gift card! Now I could buy the new outfit I'd been wanting! "Well, actually I am available in the evenings or on Saturday," I responded.

"Pick a time here, and we will hold a reservation for you," he informed me.

"Carrie, what are you getting into?" Katie scolded.

"Katie, I can buy an outfit with a $100 gift card! It's worth it to me," I said.

"You know they'll try to sell a timeshare to you, do you think you can resist?" Katie teased.

"Of course, I couldn't afford one anyway!" I chanted.

Katie asked, "Hey, do you have anymore coupons for the Chinese restaurant we went to? That was really good and I wanted to go back later this week," Katie said.

"No, that was the last one, but I have a lot of other coupons for other restaurants if you want to look at those," I offered.

"Thanks, maybe I'll take a look," she responded. You know, you really ARE the coupon queen!"

"Carrie?" Katie asked tentatively.

"Yea," I replied.

"Don't you think it's time to start thinking about a house? You keep saying that it's getting really tough on the girls to share a bedroom. What do you think?" Katie probed.

"Maybe, but I just don't think I can afford it," I gushed.

"You never know unless you try, let me know if you want to go looking at houses together. I love to do that!" Katie emphasized.

"Thanks for the support, Katie, I really appreciate your faith in me," I relayed.

Maybe Katie was right.

Maybe it was time to start thinking about getting a house. God, help me!

CHAPTER 25

MORE EMBRACES

I was back at camp in Santa Cruz. It was the fall of 1998.

This time I was at the camp for a spiritual growth retreat. I pondered how I never would have imagined that I could be so embraced in my new life. I found a world that I didn't know existed full of people from a myriad of life circumstances that had thrust them into singlehood.

My perspective shifted into a much broader place than I'd ever been before. I was becoming less judgmental. My eyes were opened to understanding in ways they never had been before.

Just when I thought life was becoming more settled.

Jerry showed up.

He found me in the lodge where I was eating. He asked if we could talk. My heart was stirring with familiar flutters that screamed, "You are my heart's desire, it's been too long that you've been away."

We walked out past the meadow beyond the bridge where the creek ran, to a bench that was near the outdoor chapel in the woods. It was one of my favorite places, and one of the few open spaces in the dense grounds where redwood trees and giant ferns grew in abundance.

"How have you been?" he asked.

"Good, yourself?" I shyly replied.

"Great, just wanted to do some catching up," he responded.

Jerry had a quiet reserve about him that was different than when we had crossed paths in the past. I presumed that he was fighting to control his emotions. He had told me several years back that he would spend every night fantasizing about me and longing for me to be with him, in spite of knowing that I was married and not wanting to interfere with that. I also knew that his heart had been taken with me as much as mine with him. I wondered how he thought about us now.

I decided to take a risk, "So, are you dating?" I inquired.

"Yes, in fact, I was with someone for over a year," he sighed. My mind quickly counted backwards to when they may have stopped dating. *Why didn't he reach out to me when I became available?* I ached.

He seemed to read my mind because he continued with, "I wrestled with whether to contact you after I broke up my last relationship. I decided against it because there was so much physical distance between us. I couldn't see myself commuting in your direction and I thought it wouldn't be good for you to come my direction either. You have your girls to think about and your teaching job."

"Besides that, I have an old house, and worn out furniture. You know I don't make much money in my job. You probably make more money than me. I think you want more than that. You deserve more than that. I just think I couldn't make you happy with what I have," he admitted painfully.

So, the old male ego rears its head.

He continued, "We were very attracted to each other and I felt very close to you, but the truth is that we didn't really know each other in our everyday worlds. I like hard rock music, and maybe you don't prefer that. You probably like things I don't like. We don't even know what we like to watch on television. I am a very strict parent, and you might not like how I would deal with your girls."

As he talked, my heart was sinking. I had always held out hope that one day his situation would change so that he was available, and that perhaps we could be together. I could see that perhaps that wasn't going to be the case. *Maybe he was right, maybe it wasn't meant to be.* I found it interesting, however, that when I was finally available, he didn't seem interested.

"There's something else," he admitted. "I have felt really guilty and I don't think I could handle being together. I don't think I helped your marriage by being attracted and responding to you. Now that you're divorced, I really feel badly."

"It's not your fault, Jerry, because there were a lot of things going south in my marriage before you and I connected. In fact, you probably helped me stay in the marriage longer than I might have been able to, had you not helped to support me," I added, sincerely.

"Thank you for saying that, but I still have my own feelings to deal with, besides, I'm with Barbara now," he confessed.

Huh? Where had that come from? "For real, Jerry, you are with someone else, again?" I asked, slightly agitated.

"Yea, and I'm very happy," he smiled.

"Then I'm happy for you," I lied.

We made small talk and I told him about what the girls were doing, and the plans I had for the holidays. I asked about his kids, who were in high school, much older than mine. He talked about the coastline and how beautiful it is in the fall. His work had been keeping him busy sixty hours a week, and he liked it that way. "That's another thing that you wouldn't like," he said, "I work very long hours."

He's clearly trying to keep emotional distance, I thought. Probably doesn't want to hurt again. He must have gone through a lot when his wife died, then he became emotionally attached to me, an unavailable married woman. Poor guy. He's protecting himself. I understood.

Jerry was probably right. It was a very long distance between us, and our lives were very different. No, I didn't like hard rock music. No, I wouldn't like him working sixty hours a week. And teenagers? I wouldn't know where to start in dealing with them! My girls were not there yet. I am probably more lax in parenting than he is. We would clash.

The rest of the weekend I tried to wrap my head around the words that Jerry shared. I guess it's time to let go, once again, I admitted to myself. It wasn't going to be easy. Who else could I fall back on? It was God and I as partners on the road of life. Thank goodness for the girls. Thank goodness for Katie.

Given the chance, I couldn't help but wonder what it could have been like with Jerry. We never got a chance to play it out. There were so many frustrated desires and fantasies. Maybe that's all they were, fantasies.

I knew I wanted to be rescued and that it was probably not in my best interests to be thinking that way. I needed to stay on a path of healing. I needed to keep developing myself and discover more about myself and who I was. I completely lost touch with myself in my marriage. I couldn't leap back into another relationship before I had those questions answered, *could I?*

I could feel myself weaken with the passing of time. It was hard being a single mom. It was hard being the only breadwinner. It was hard taking care of everyday responsibilities and being the only parent. I was tired. Sometimes I just wanted someone to lean on and give me a break!

As I packed up, Jerry passed me in the hallway, took hold of my arm and whipped me into the nearby cabin. With a full frontal embrace, he locked lips with me in a passionate kiss that lasted a full minute, at least.

"I've wanted to do that for a very long time," he revealed. *That person is still in there. It's just that too much time has passed*, I considered.

My head was dizzy as I walked away, thoughts ricocheting like popcorn, popping about aimlessly. *That's odd, after all this time of longing, the kiss was not what I thought it would be.* I filed it away to re-consider later.

Was it possible to have a physical attraction that is created only in the mind and not reality?

CHAPTER 26

ANYTHING'S POSSIBLE

In my new life, I found that I continued to be blessed, beyond my wildest expectations. After living in the apartment for three years, the girls became very restless and started talking about living in a house again. How could I tell them I didn't have the money? The three of us started a very focused prayer, for a house. The girls prayed for a swimming pool. I said, "What if my prayer is to NOT have a swimming pool?" We realized we had to be "in sync" in order to make things happen. On a Saturday morning I received a phone call from a male friend. He asked, "Who is this?"

I said, "What do you mean, who is this, you called me, remember?"

He said, "Oh, sorry, I was cleaning out my wallet and came across your number, and I was trying to remember who you were. This is Trent."

Thanks a lot.

We continued the conversation anyway. He told me that he was a real estate agent, and was I, by any chance, looking for a house? While he talked, I searched my memory to figure out who this person was. Oh, he was the man I had spoken to at a single's dance. He was the one drawing his "dream house" on a napkin. He had told me he wanted a stream running through the backyard, and if he had his way, it would be located in Chesapeake Bay. He had dark hair and dark eyes, and a very thick crop of hair, and was of a very solid build. I'd say he was about six feet tall. He was interesting enough, I thought.

My mind switched back to the present moment. Indeed I was looking for a house. He arranged to get together to show me properties. I warned him that I didn't have much money. He assured me that there were "special programs" for people in my situation.

I trusted him, and kept moving forward with my trusting in the future seed of faith.

Not long afterwards, a check came in the mail.

Years before, while we lived in Fairfield, we had signed a petition that was going around the neighborhood. You know one of those things someone brings to your doorstep, on a clipboard? It was a lawsuit that the neighborhood was pursuing because of a chemical plant that had gone in behind us, causing health ailments for some. I signed, thinking, *That's the last I'll see of this.*

Here was a check, for $8,000 from that lawsuit from so many years before. I nearly fell over from shock. *How had they gotten my new address?* And, how had it arrived in such a timely manner, now, when I needed it the most? It turned out that $4000 went to our investor, $2000 to Mark, and $2000 to myself. In addition to the "special program," it was just the amount I needed for a down payment.

We were looking for a house during a time when there were multiple offers on houses. The week we were looking to buy was no exception. Trent negotiated with the owner to consider me as the more desirable occupant. He painted a picture of me as a desperate single mom who needed a place more than anyone else. It must have worked, because the offer was accepted.

Not only was the offer accepted, but the owner left gardening tools, refrigerator, washer and dryer and lots of other useful items that came in handy and were greatly appreciated. *Thank you Trent, and thank you God. Thank you Katie for encouraging me.*

The house we bought was perfect for our needs with a pomegranate tree, lemon tree, and lots of rosebushes. I would be able to garden once more. We had three bedrooms, one for each of us.

Even though there was only one bathroom, we would manage. There was a huge backyard, with lots of room for the girls to sprawl. There was a large covered patio that provided lots of shade. There was even a separate living room and family room, almost nonexistent in the small homes in this neighborhood. It was more than I thought we would be able to afford, and I was very grateful.

Trent became my boyfriend and helped with repairs on the house. He was very handy and creative and even helped with decorating. He told me he had grown up in a poor neighborhood down south and learned to make things from garbage dumps. He had pieced together metal pieces to make himself a bicycle. Impressive, I thought. He picked up relics at garage sales with my house in mind. He found a wide crescent-shaped basket with a narrow depth that he suggested could be hung on the wall with a plant draped over its side. The next thing I knew he was bringing over an empty plastic carton that fit perfectly inside that could be used as the planter.

It seemed he thought of things before I could even ask. He thinned out ferns from his yard and brought them over to plant off my patio. He did the same thing with lilies. Along the back fence he built a frame to steady grape vines that were planted alongside it. He hacked down the lemon tree when it died and was no longer fruitful. He taught me how to take care of maintenance items when the need arose.

The house was over fifty years old and needed a lot of work. When the gas and electric bill arrived with $300 due, he offered to go into the crawl space underneath the house to wrap the pipes with insulation to save on energy costs. When a water pipe sprang a leak in the backyard, he came over at 1:00 in the morning to fix it.

I'd finally found someone to rescue me.

There were things that were really starting to bother me, however.

"I brought a pine tree over to plant in the front yard," Trent announced.

"Where will you put it, there is already a big tree there," I said perplexedly.

"This one will go on the side, a ways from the other one, it will be fine," he argued.

Why wasn't he listening to me? Wasn't it my yard, not his?! This began to eat away at me.

It wasn't the first time he hadn't listened to me.

Another time Erin, Kayla, Trent and I were playing a game and he started acting like an immature child. He began verbally poking at Kayla and got in a disagreement. When she pushed back at him, he marked her arm with a marker. This didn't go over very well with either of the girls. I didn't like it either. He didn't seem to think there was anything wrong with his actions.

Trent seemed to be drawing into himself more and more. When he was responsive, it was in a flat tone, with little emotion. It became harder to relate to him. He finally made it known that he was depressed and taking an anti-depressant. With this new information, my guilt kicked in for wanting to be away from him.

Not too much later, he shared that an old girlfriend told him that he'd been seen sitting outside her house late at night, and that he did not remember having done that. "In fact," he said, "sometimes I wake up in the morning and find a lot more miles on my speedometer than there were before I went to bed. I think I might be driving around at night and not remembering it."

With that, I decided for sure, that we had to break up. It was just a matter of when and how. I started to get really scared. I was scared for the girls too. *Was he not safe? I didn't want to put any of us at risk.*

It would be some time before I figured out how to carry this out. He was still a steady companion that I wasn't quite ready to let go of.

In the fall of 2001, I knew it was time.

I told him over the phone when he got a little more stable with his depression. I surveyed the outside with trepidation. I wanted to make sure that he was not going to stalk me or the girls. I never saw him at my house again.

I had to move on and let go, once again.

CHAPTER 27

NEW TRADITIONS

As the decision-maker and head of household, I found that ideas were coming to me that I'd never considered before. *I wonder why we never had many traditions in our family with Mark?* I guess he was consumed with his illness, and so it would have been up to me. *I didn't take that role, so it didn't happen.* It jumped out at me now, as I considered the possibilities.

One of the things I felt a need for, was to somehow establish a peaceful home. We had so many conflicts, that I wanted to create more harmony. I wasn't sure how to go about it, but I kept it in my mind and heart and meditated on it.

It was Erin who approached me with the idea of putting a garden in the middle of our yard. She had watched a television show that demonstrated a circular fountain, surrounded by floral décor. I suggested that the middle of the yard might not be the best place for a garden. I was thinking of how difficult it would be to mow, and the fact that we would lose the open space we now had.

Over time, the idea grew on me and I realized that the garden could go at the end of the patio, under the large maple tree that provided an abundance of shade. A fountain would cost a lot of money, I considered. How was I going to do that?

The thought occurred to me again, a short time later while I attended a home and garden show. There in front of the entrance were fountains and the cutest "bunny" steps. I eyed a stone bench in the same design. Those would be perfect, I thought. Considering the sale price, the cost wasn't too outrageous. What I neglected to realize was how heavy the stone fountain and bench would be to unload. The sales clerk loaded the items into my car, and the car sunk low to the ground. I do mean low, way low. That was my first clue.

My second clue was the fact that I could not transport them when I got home. With a wheelbarrow and my neighbor's help, the pieces were lifted out, and carried to the backyard. This is a lot of work, I began to realize more fully.

The garden became my new project. I carefully picked out a low-lying groundcover to fill in the spaces between the bunny steps. The fountain was placed in the center of the squared-off space allotted for the garden. The steps were set in rows shooting off in four segments from the fountain, like spokes of a wheel. It's beginning to look like a garden, I noticed with pride.

The girls assisted in the beginning stages by clearing grass and weeds. They lost interest soon afterwards in putting the garden together. They were busy with other endeavors. That's OK, I thought, they'll appreciate it when it's done. Somewhere deep within, I think I needed to do the work. It was healing for me.

In a series of steps, the garden began to take shape. After loosening the dirt, the topsoil was added (and I do mean LOTS). As I laid each step, and planted each plant, I felt my life taking shape and getting back on track. This was such a peaceful place, I hoped it could help us create harmony in our home too. After much work and planning, the garden was beginning to share it's blessings back with us.

Birds and squirrels started to play in the fountain and frolic on the steps. In spite of the work, it had been well worth it. Besides the obvious beauty, I realized another reason it had been so important for me to wade through the process of creating the garden.

I wanted the girls to see the benefit of investing time, energy, money and planning into a worthwhile project. I wanted them to see that they could create anything they want for themselves. It had become something beautiful through our efforts and was now giving back to us the joy of peace and quiet and a place to enjoy the beauty of nature. It was indeed our peace garden, which I had envisioned.

We had successfully transformed the grassy patch into an area more beautiful than what we started with. I wanted the girls to know that they are creators of beauty, peace, success, love, and anything else beautiful they choose to bring into their life. I wanted them to know they create their own destiny by the choices they make each day.

With money being tight, I wanted to show the girls that we could also create what we wanted for ourselves, even though it might be different than what they were initially thinking. At Christmastime, we bought one new game a year. The girls loved to play games during the holidays and wanted the newest ones. Purchasing one a year was more financially feasible and it became a tradition they looked forward to.

In addition, the electronic age was fully upon us and ads were constantly pleading with onlookers to buy the latest rage. Erin and Kayla were definitely part of the onlookers. In addition to the games, I decided to gift the family one larger purchase each year during the holidays. Consequently, we purchased a VCR one year, and a karaoke machine with accompanying CD's the following year. They each still received individual gifts, but it became a way we could share as a family as well.

As the girls grew older, they each received "future gifts," to add to their needs for items that would be useful when they lived on their own. One year, it was sewing machines. Another year it became the Bible with their names engraved on them. They enthusiastically embraced the new traditions and began voicing their gift wishes and ideas when the holidays approached.

Traditions were established around mealtimes as well. Erin had one night to choose a menu for dinner. Kayla had a different night she chose her preference. We would eat out one night a week, or bring in take-out. The girls clung to the security they felt from the consistent implementation of these customs and it seemed to ease the pain of transitioning between two homes.

That first year in our new home I was anxious to offer them even more.

CHAPTER 28

SANTA'S PET MAIL EXPRESS

C hristmas Eve 1999 Santa left a creative invitation in Erin and Kayla's stockings. As Santa's helper, I wanted to continue doing what I could to make a comfortable home for them.

This is how it read:

This contract, upon your signature agreeing to the terms herewith, is good for one pet of your choice. All family members must be accepting of the chosen pet (especially head honcho). The pet may be a kitty, puppy (to grow to a small dog only), bunny, bird, or other acceptable choice.

Conditions of this agreement:
1. Give daily and weekly care as needed.
2. Provide for care of the pet if you are gone three or more days, or if your head honcho is going to be out of town.
3. Take the pet with you when you leave home.

Care to include:
1. Daily feeding, walking, poop clean-up, letting in/out of the house, and training.

2. Weekly cleanings (bathing, nail and hair clippings).

Consequences of neglect:

1. Occasional neglect will result in loss of allowance for that week.
2. More than occasional neglect will mean permanent loss of allowance.
3. On-going failure to assume responsibility will result in return of animal to the Animal Rescue Foundation.

Pet will be returned under these conditions:

1. Destruction of people or property by the pet.
2. Neglectful care by the owner.
3. Allergies or other health or safety issues for any family member.
4. Expense becomes too great for head honcho.

No pet will be acquired in haste. You must look at and experience several kinds of pets before you choose. A final decision will not be made before January 31st. A puppy or kitty will be acquired through pet connection with Animal Rescue Foundation only, where the cost is free.

YOU HAVE THE OPTION OF VOIDING THIS CONTRACT BY CHOOSING NO PET AND RECEIVING $25 BY HEAD HONCHO INSTEAD, WITHIN THE NEXT 30 DAYS.

I agree to the conditions of the contract, as stated herewith.

_____   _____

Your Signature   Date

Mark refused to consider having a pet when we were married, so Santa and his helper took the opportunity to extend this invitation in our new home.

"So what do you think of the contract?" I asked as I peered into the living room where the girls were pulling out their stocking goods.

"Awesome," Erin replied, "I want a cat, can I get a cat?"

"Did you read the contract?" I asked, making sure she had considered everything before she was deciding.

"Yes," she exuberantly exclaimed.

"I want $25 Mom, because I don't think I'm ready to walk a dog and all the other things that need to be done," Kayla piped in her reply.

"That's very thoughtful," I observed, "are you sure you don't want a puppy, Kayla?"

"No I'm not ready for all that, and a puppy and kitty wouldn't get along anyway," she added.

What a mature response, I thought, *I hope she's not relinquishing what she wants because Erin said she wants a cat.*

"Well, think about it some more, both of you," I suggested. A cat hmm, that would be interesting. I've never had a cat before. I hope I'll know how to help take care of it, I reflected.

It turned out they were both set on their decisions and Erin brought home Hazel, a green eyed, caramel-colored charmer. Kayla and I laughed, because Hazel was a him. He had been in the wild. He was muscle-bound enough that he could leap from the floor to the top of the refrigerator, and make it look effortless. Erin carried him around like a baby. Kayla enjoyed him too, until she got scratched, and then decided to keep her distance.

Hazel began seeking me out in my room and curling up next to me, offering his comfort and warmth. He conveyed a sixth sense that was becoming more apparent as time passed by. He slipped into my room and into my heart without my noticing. Whenever I felt the slightest bit down, he found his way next to me, or in my lap. I noticed he did the same for Erin and Kayla, but they weren't always so welcoming of his sharp-clawed toes, or nipping at their things.

In January of the following year, Erin held Hazel in the car while I drove to the vet's for his vaccinations. Following the ordeal, she asked to be taken to her dad's because it was her day to visit. As she stepped out of the car, she held onto Hazel and announced, "I'm just going to hold him on the grass for a minute, he'll like it."

"Are you sure it's a good idea?" I questioned her.

"It'll be fine, Mom," and as soon as the words left her mouth, Hazel was crouching to get ready to lunge. "Mom," she screamed, "help me!" she exclaimed.

I ran around to the other side of the car to come to her rescue, but it was too late, Hazel charged off into the brush before I could lend a hand. A look of terror, desperation and remorse reflected on her face as she went racing after him.

"Mom, I don't see him," she screamed in further desperation.

I ran to her side to aide in the search. We saw no sign of him but kept marching to where it appeared he could be hiding. After a short time, Erin realized the gravity of the situation and broke down. "We'll never find him, Mom," she blurted out. All of the pain of the past few years came pouring out, as I held her and felt the pain and anguish with her.

We kept looking the best we could, without a clear trail to follow. It became more and more hopeless as the minutes passed. We didn't want to give up. I drove around the neighborhood to get a better view from the other side. Still no luck.

The next three weeks were spent driving around in the damp fog with the car window down, calling for Hazel. It was winter in January of the year 2000. I ended up with pneumonia that lasted for another three weeks. Lying in my bed, delirious with fever, I heard paws scratching my door. *Was that Hazel? He always scratched my door to let me know he wanted in.* Then I remembered that he was gone. Perhaps he was dead, and he was coming back to visit me in the spirit. I wasn't sure. I called nearby veterinary hospitals giving his description. There was one cat that fit his description, who had been in an accident and later died. It was too late for me to confirm that it was Hazel. He was no longer at the hospital, they informed me. I would never know. He was not to be found.

I was suffering from yet another broken heart.

CHAPTER 29

FINDING MY WAY

Guess it's up to me now, I decided. The hardest part is getting things done around the house, I painstakingly acknowledged.

"Katie, what do you do when you need things done around your house?" I inquired.

"Well, I ask a boyfriend, but if I don't have one, I hire a fix-it man," she elaborated.

"Just by looking in the phone book?" I pressed further.

"Yep," she declared.

"Thanks, Katie, you're always so helpful," I responded.

"No problem, hey, we're still going to the Presbyterian Single's Group activity on Sunday, right?" she reminded me.

"Wouldn't miss it," I agreed.

"Maybe our guys will be there," she quipped.

"Maybe so," I fired back.

Katie and I each had our eye out for men we had spotted at the last meeting. We never knew who would show up because it changed every week. That's what made it exciting, with an element of mystery.

I had dated a little bit, but was still working on getting over Trent. He'd called me periodically trying to get back together. I was holding firm, because I didn't see it going anywhere. I think it's been better this way.

My mind drifted back to the house and what needed to be done. I had to get a cat door put in the garage door so that Hazel, our new pet, could get back and forth to his litter box in the garage. I guess I better have the fireplace fixed too, I remembered. When the house was inspected, the inspector told me that the metal doors in the chimney were rusted and difficult to open. I sure didn't want to use the fireplace and have smoke backfire so that we would be suffocating. There was so much to think about, I realized.

My fingers flipped through the phone book until they landed on "Handyman Services." That's what I want. I wonder which one to choose? Probably a smaller company won't cost as much, I calculated. Best to call a number of different choices and compare them, I further considered.

"Frank's Fix-It All," a robust voice announced.

"Hi, I'm looking for a general fix-it person to help with some repairs on my house," I informed him.

"Well, we don't do much with general, but we can help you with specific jobs you may need help with," he mused.

So, a funny guy, I like that, surely he is safe, I quickly evaluated.

"What have you got going on?" he continued.

"I need to have a cat door put in, and the chute covering in my fireplace fixed," I carefully explained.

"We can do that," he chirped.

"What is your hourly rate?" I asked, hoping for something I could afford.

"We charge $20/hour, plus parts," he elaborated.

That's the most reasonable quote I've gotten, I realized. *Shouldn't I get referrals*, or check them out on Better Business Bureau? I pondered.

"When could you do the work?" I further inquired.

"Let's see, we have time this Wednesday at 1:00 p.m.," he stated.

"That would work, can we schedule that?" I pleaded.

"OK, it's on the calendar. Just give me your address," he requested.

"1088 Peculiar Street," I shared.

"Got it, see you on Wednesday," he confirmed.

After I got off the phone I went straight to Better Business Bureau in the phone book and made the call. It seemed to check out okay. There's probably nothing to worry about, I assured myself.

Wednesday arrived quickly. The girls were occupied watching a Mary Kate and Ashley video.

"My name's Frank, from Frank's Fix-It?" he reminded me.

"Oh, I wasn't expecting Frank himself," I laughed.

"I have a small business, so I'm the only employee, except for one other person who helps me from time to time," he elaborated.

"Oh, that's fine," I confirmed, as I stepped aside for him to come inside.

I didn't expect him to be so cute either, I observed. He was tall, probably over six feet. He had sandy, wavy hair and broad shoulders. His eyes are what caught my attention first, dancing green eyes, the kind that look like they have lots of fun.

I don't think I was too far off, as he proceeded to joke with me while he was working.

"So, you're a single mom?" he probed.

Should I tell him? Where was the line here? I didn't know him. He was basically a stranger.

"Well, sort of," I skirted around his question.

The longer he worked, the more I stared at his hot body, first in the family room lying face down making a cat door, then in the living room, with his backside protruding feet first out of the fireplace. The more he joked playfully with me, the more I warmed up and began to think of him more as a friend. By the time he left he knew I lived alone with the girls, was divorced, among handfuls of other personal information. *Was I crazy?*

In spite of the bells of caution ringing in my head, I agreed to go on a date with him.

He arrived a little late, pulling up in a BMW. He announced, "Could we take your car 'cause my beamer has to go to the shop, I probably shouldn't even have driven it this far."

"In fact," he continued, "if you could follow me down the street to the yogurt shop I'd like to leave my car there."

"The yogurt shop? Why there?" I questioned him.

"My uncle owns it. This way, my car will already be there when we get back and he can take me home," he explained.

"Your uncle will be there late?" I further questioned him. That's odd for a yogurt shop to be open late, I considered.

"Yep," he responded.

My brain was racing faster than the engine in my Mazda RX-7. *If I drive, at least I can be in control and won't have to worry about whether he's a safe driver. I don't like that this is a date and I'm paying for the gas. I'm definitely not paying for the meal!* I had an uneasy feeling, but I couldn't see a reason for not going. I would be the driver.

We started at Buffalo Bill's to eat dinner. At least he had asked me where I wanted to go, I thought. Maybe he's not so bad after all. Because there was no seating available in the main restaurant, we ended up sitting in the lounge area.

"So what kinds of things do you like to do, Carrie?" he inquired.

I like that he's interested in me, I considered. "I love to read, travel, do crafts, all kinds of things," I bounced back.

"Where do you like to travel?" he probed further.

"My favorite travel is down south. I love the San Diego area. I enjoy visiting my family in the Midwest too, but if I just want to relax I prefer the warmer weather," I explained.

"San Diego is great," he agreed.

"What about you, Frank, where do you like to go?" I asked.

"I don't get to travel much because I work long hours, because it's only me. I work a lot of weekends and can't really afford to take vacations. Maybe after my business is built up a little more I'll be able to take time off," he elaborated.

"So your business is fairly new?" I questioned.

"Yes, my whole family is in The Mafia." HUH?! I must have made frog eyes, because he hesitated before continuing. Did I hear what I thought I heard? Surely not! "Don't worry, I'm not in it anymore," he continued. WHAT?! HE was in The Mafia too?!

His voice faded to my hearing as I desperately began searching around the room for the nearest exit. *Maybe I would need to run out of here! Did he have a gun? What was going to happen?* The alarm bells that were ringing in my head earlier were now gongs resonating so loudly that I felt dizzy.

His voice alerted me back to reality. Yes, he really was seated across from me.

". . . . I wanted to get out of The Mafia, but I still had to have a way of making a living. That was several years ago," he shared.

"I live with my dad in Susuin City. He's a millionaire and I'm the only heir in his will," he boasted. A fleeting twinge of excitement leaped into my chest, but was quickly squashed by my more reasonable self.

I don't want any part of this, I thought. I've got to get away from him, but how?

We left the restaurant and when he asked where we should go next, I suggested dancing, because I was thinking if I wanted to end the evening too early he would get suspicious and what, be angry? I didn't know, but I didn't want to rock any boats, or any ex-Mafia members either.

As soon as I could get away with an excuse to end the evening, I took it. The dance hall we went to wasn't appealing to either one of us. I said I was tired and ready to go. He didn't argue.

I never saw him again.

Thank goodness.

After that incident I was a lot more careful with my choices. *Better safe than sorry.*

There didn't seem to be anything unsafe about continuing to frequent timeshare presentations to collect on free vacations, gift cards, and cash. It was my new hobby. I had accumulated quite a wardrobe from Macy's as a result of my freebies. I made a habit of being honest when they asked questions, so I thought there was nothing wrong with it.

Sunrise Travel was my favorite, so when they called I jumped at the chance to go to a presentation.

"Carrie, your representative is waiting for you in the video room," the receptionist announced.

Well, it was my turn. Probably the same old thing, first a video, then a salesman pressuring me to buy their timeshare after giving me a rundown on what they have to offer. I should be out of here in another hour or so. Sometimes they give me the gift early when I tell them upfront I have no intention of buying.

"George's my name," the salesman conveyed to me, after the video ended. "What did you think?" he continued.

"Very nice," I replied.

He led me to a small round table with a couple of resort books piled on one side. I spotted a snack table on the other side of the room. He must have noticed my attention diverting in that direction because he said, "Oh, can I get you something?" he asked. "In fact, go and help yourself, I'll meet you back here."

"Thanks," I said.

I came back to the table to find that he had left, so I sat down and started eating. When he returned, he had a stressed look on his face. "Do you know you've been here six times before?" he spewed.

"Oh, is that right? I haven't been counting. You're the ones who called me, remember? I figured you kept track of that. If you didn't want me back here, I guess I assumed you wouldn't call," I flung back.

"We won't be calling you again," he stated curtly.

"Well, guess I'll have to buy my timeshare somewhere else," I quipped.

"Go show the registration form at the desk to get your gift," he jabbed.

"Thanks," I stated politely.

Maybe the sand was running out in the hourglass.

CHAPTER 30

SAYING GOODBYE

Dear Carrie:

Continue to move forward and feel the freedom that is yours. As you continue to take steps, you will feel your new pathway, and know in your heart who and how a companion can walk with you. Trust in the things that you feel. My assurance will rest with you, if you will continue to walk with me.

Love,
Your Heavenly Father

I was back in Dr. Stewart's office. It was April 2002. I had been in therapy for seven long years. Five of those years were with Dr. Stewart.

"So this is our last session, how do you feel about that?" Dr. Stewart asked.

"I feel OK, I think I'm ready," I responded, "I just hope I can remember what I've learned and be able to put it into practice."

"So what is it that you've learned?" she inquired.

"I learned that I need to keep my focus on my feelings and myself, instead of on other people for one thing," I replied.

"How will you do that?" she asked softly. *Was she actually sad we were ending our time together?*

"By stopping and looking inside for what I want, what I feel, and what I need, instead of always going along with what people around me want," I said again.

"Like in your relationships?" she asked.

"Yes, especially my intimate relationships," I chose my words carefully.

"You've also suggested that I tend to not show how I'm feeling, but instead show indifference on the outside," I further stated.

"Do you agree with that?" she asked.

"I could see how that's probably true," I agreed. "It's not easy, because it takes courage and sometimes I get afraid."

"Afraid of what?" she inquired.

"Afraid of putting myself on the line, afraid of anger, afraid of what others might think, afraid to be me," I added.

"That's a lot of fear," she reflected.

"Yes, I'm going to practice letting go and reassure myself that it's OK to be me. If someone doesn't like me for who I am, I need to move on," I rationalized.

"I remember what you said about expressing myself in the moment too," I continued, "I'm going to remember to just keep breathing if difficult emotions start to come up, and try to express the feelings directly instead of reacting to the other person. That's the hardest part. There's still a lot of old stuff inside me that gets touched upon, especially when someone is expressing anger. I freeze up."

"Yes, we've worked a lot on that. You've gotten better at being in the moment haven't you?" she probed.

"Yes, a lot better than I used to be. Thank you for helping me with that," I shared.

"That's what I'm here for, but let's get back to you," she pushed.

"What are you going to take with you from all of the dating relationships you've been in? You could write quite a soap opera," she laughed.

I liked that she sincerely enjoyed me. I joined in the laughter. "The most important thing I've learned is that if I want to meet someone who likes me for me, then I have to be more myself. The men I've met at dances only see me all dressed up and care only what I look like. They don't see or know the real me," I painfully admitted.

"Does that mean you won't be going to anymore dances?" she clarified.

"Well, no, just that I won't focus on meeting someone there that I can build a meaningful relationship with. Family is important to me, and solid values, and spirituality," I continued.

"Where will you meet someone like that?" she probed.

"I'm not sure, church maybe, or my everyday world," I responded.

"What else have you learned?" she continued to probe.

"Wow, lots, people can be very different on the outside than on the inside, that it takes a really long time to get to know a person for who they really are, that trust takes a long time to build, for starters," I answered.

"What did you learn from Trent?" she asked.

"I learned that a person's background is very important. It never goes away. He is very gifted and wise, but there were some hidden land mines, with all the places he had inside that were unhealed. He scared me and I don't think I could have fixed him," I explained.

"That's important too, huh? To not go into a relationship trying to fix someone," she repeated.

"Yes," and "I've learned it's OK to be more assertive and express myself, kinda like I already said, only I can't be afraid of it," I reiterated.

"Like you were afraid in your marriage?" she clarified.

"Yes, and I was too dependent. I needed to learn to do things for myself, and think for myself, instead of always allowing Mark to make decisions and take the lead," I asserted.

"Is that part of the reason you get scared now, because you're afraid of getting back in the same kind of situation?" she questioned.

"Yes, I think so, but I have to remind myself that I am in control of my own life. I know I was co-dependent and I'm working on getting more independent," I relayed.

"How do you think you were co-dependent?" she pressed further.

"Taking care of others more than myself, thinking that I wasn't worth having my needs met, not being myself, and honest with myself or allowing myself to feel my feelings," I said.

"Maybe not setting boundaries and then suffering because of it?" she added.

"Yes, I'm working on that one," I replied.

"I know it will be an ongoing struggle at times, but I think I have the tools now to take with me to deal with situations as they occur," I said.

"I think you're much stronger now too," she conceded.

"Anything else you want to talk about today?" she inquired.

"I was wondering if I would be able to come back sometime if I felt I needed to talk again?" I considered.

"The door is always open," she responded supportively.

"Carrie, how's it going with Erin and Kayla?" she asked.

"Pretty good I think," I responded, "I think many of my challenges are the same, learning to be able to express myself in the moment from within instead of reacting, and keeping boundaries. Those are the same challenges teachers have," I laughed.

"It's not easy," she agreed.

"Erin's a junior in high school, so she only has one more year to go. She's talking about being a doctor. Knowing her, she'll get there. She has a lot of drive. She's not only been going to school, but she works long hours every week at her job too. Kayla's a 6th grader now. Since she got asthma last year it has been tough, but I know she'll rise above it. She hasn't had any incidents for a whole year. She's really talented too. She's a natural-born swimmer, and loves to be creative, whether it's singing or drawing or writing. I can't wait to see what career direction their lives take," I shared enthusiastically.

"So what's next for you?" she queried. "This summer I'm taking classes towards getting my Education Specialist Credential. I told you I'm a special education teacher now, didn't I?" I asked.

"Yes, that's exciting, I admire you that you are going back to school after all the classes you've already taken," she replied.

"Seems like that's the fate of teachers," I continued, "I got my master's degree about fifteen years ago and I think I've been taking classes ever since!" I laughed.

She chuckled. "So back to your plan, what about your more personal goals?" she probed.

"Find a man, of course," I laughed again. "Seriously, for the first time I don't feel like I need anyone. It would be nice, but I feel like I am getting very independent and I'm OK by myself.

"That must feel like a good place to be," she smiled.

"It feels great," I acknowledged, "but I am still keeping open to possibilities."

"That's a healthy attitude," she affirmed.

"You've done a lot of internal work to get to this place, you can be really proud of yourself. I remember a year ago when you wanted to stop coming," she suggested.

"Yea, and you pushed hard at me to get me to go deeper and stick around," I interrupted.

"Are you glad you did?" she asked.

"Definitely, it has probably been the work I've done during this past year that has helped me the most, so thank you," I whispered.

"You're welcome, but again, that's my job," she reiterated.

"Oh, I almost forgot, I got a card in the mail from Jerry last week," I stated.

"And?" she inquired.

"He told me that he got married over Easter," I replied.

"How do you feel about that?" she probed.

"I was caught by surprise, but realized that he would be moving forward sometime, since he let me know he couldn't be with me," I said.

"I'm glad for him on one hand, and sad for myself on another level," I admitted.

"Sad how?" she asked.

"Sad that we can never be and that the door is definitely closed for good," my words spilled out.

"I'm sorry, I do wish you the best, but our time is up," she replied glibly.

"Good-bye," I said. She gave me a hug.

I am getting strong and independent.

I don't need to have a man, but I am getting tired of having to always say good-bye.

CHAPTER 31

WANNA KARAOKE?

It was June 2002.

It was 3:00 on Sunday afternoon. I had just enough time to go to the grocery store before meeting Katie at the Presbyterian Single's group meeting. I would have to make it quick so that I would have time to get dinner for the girls. They would be back from their dad's at 4:00. They enjoyed sharing some time with me before I would be leaving. I hesitated to go the meetings every week because it took me away from the girls more than I liked. I don't think they liked me being gone every week either.

Let's see, I need green beans to go with the macaroni and cheese, oh and peanut butter for the celery sticks. It was one of our favorite meals. Canned apricots topped off the meal that had become one of our staples. It was easy for me to fix and they were happy. I didn't like them having too much white flour from the noodles, or sugar from the syrup in the apricots, so I had started buying sugar-free syrup and multi-grain noodles. So far, so good. They hadn't noticed the changes.

It was really hard to cook healthy all the time when I was so tired from working full-time and trying to keep up with my credential classes. Sometimes I gave in and let them have pizza. I know I shouldn't, but it was just too much to cook full meals every night. I would keep trying, because I knew healthy foods were best for them.

I think I'll take a shortcut down the freezer aisle to get to the fresh foods, I thought. I turned the corner, and as I glanced up saw a great big, wide-mouthed, gleaming smile shot straight at me. He acts like he knows me. Do I know him? He does look familiar but I don't know where I've seen him. I won't say anything, I don't want to sound stupid, I thought.

He has a nice smile. I wonder if I'll see him again, I pondered, as I left the store to head back home.

I arrived just in time to greet the girls in the doorway. I loved getting their "glad to be back home" hugs. Sometimes they were grouchy, though, when returning home. I think it was their way of letting me know they didn't like having to go back and forth. They were expected to be more independent at their dad's too, and I think that was hard on them.

"What did you do at your dad's?"

"We went swimming, and watched TV," they echoed each other.

"Well, I'm glad to have you back home," I smiled.

"Charlotte is going to be with you for a few hours while I go to my meeting tonight," I offered carefully.

"Oh Mom, not again," Kayla whined.

"I don't need a sitter, I'm way too old for this," repeated Erin.

"I know, but it's not fair for you to have the all the responsibility while I'm gone," I explained.

"I'll be back in time for bedtime," I further explained.

"Who wants macaroni and cheese?" I diverted their attention.

"We do," Kayla chanted.

"Again, really?" Erin complained. "Can't we have something else?"

Just when I thought I was pleasing them! "I'll let you pick tomorrow night, alright, Erin?" I offered.

"Alright, I guess," she agreed, "but I work tomorrow night."

"Well then, Tuesday night," I corrected.

Upon leaving I called Katie to let her know I was on the way. She would be waiting and wondering where I was. She told me the program had just started so she would save me a seat.

I listened to meditative music on the drive, while passing the rolling green hills of the East Bay.

I love it when it's green, I thought. It reminds me of the Midwest and back home. It turns brown way too early here.

After parking, I easily spotted Katie near the back of the room. She was all smiles. She's always so cheerful, how does she do it? I wondered.

The topic for the evening was "Finding Your Soul Mate." How fitting, just what Katie and I need, even though we made great soul mate companions for each other. Katie, however, was not a man!

The information was similar to other talks I'd heard. Ideas included getting involved in activities you enjoy, being yourself, opening up and showing your feelings and thoughts, and on and on. Hmmm, sounds a lot like my counseling sessions, I realized.

After the talk we joined the crowd at the back of the room, milling around and indulging in the treats that were spread out on the table. *They look a lot like vultures coming in for a landing*, I entertained myself. You would think that singles never eat. I guess it's just more difficult cooking for one person, that's all. I think a lot of these people don't have primary care for their children, or don't have children. I need to find someone who understands my life with children, I tucked away.

"Carrie, come over here, there's someone I want you to meet," Katie signaled to me.

Katie was always the little mother, taking care of me. I do enjoy it, I must admit. She has so many friends, it's nice to have her invite me to meet many of them.

"This is Jack, the guy I played tennis with last week. Do you remember me telling you about him?" she asked.

I nodded my head in agreement. I really couldn't remember, she had so many activities and friends, so there was no use trying to keep track. I couldn't possibly keep up. I definitely didn't stay as busy socially as she did, because I was trying to put the girls first.

I know they didn't feel that way on evenings like this, when I went out. I was trying to re-balance my life. I've always put everyone else first, and never taken care of my own needs, so now I was trying to say not just to myself, but to the girls, that it's OK to think about myself sometimes too. It had been a hard transition.

My mind jolted back to the present moment with a tap on my shoulder. I turned around. There behind me was Mr. Gleaming Smile, from the grocery store. *This must be where I had seen him before. What were the odds?* I had driven at least twenty minutes to get here, and there he was at the grocery store not even a mile from my house. *Funny.*

"Didn't we just see each other at the store?" he inquired.

I laughed. "I was just thinking the same thing," I responded back.

"I think I've seen you here before," he continued.

"Oh yeah? When was that?" I probed.

"I remember," he continued, "at the Monday night parenting class, weren't you there?"

"Yes, I was there a few weeks," I agreed, "so you have kids?"

"Uh-huh, three of them, two boys and a girl," he grinned.

Three of them? Maybe that's a little stretch, God, but it was refreshing to meet someone with children who perhaps would understand the challenges of single parenting.

"Hey, could I get your phone number so we could continue this conversation?" he asked.

"Sure," I replied, "I would like that, by the way, what's your name?"

"Gary," he stated, "what's yours?"

"Carrie," I answered, "bye Gary."

"Bye, talk to you soon," he emphasized.

Katie followed me out with, "What was that?"

"It's the funniest thing, we just saw each other at the grocery store this afternoon," I reflected.

Katie hummed her musical ditty she used to indicate supernatural forces at work.

"Oh stop it, you tease, we'll see," I laughed. "He said he's got three kids."

"Well Carrie, you've already got two, what's three more?" rolled off her tongue.

I laughed again. *I would be cautious, that's for sure. I've learned my lessons from the past. What was I saying? I hadn't even gone on a date with him yet. Yet?* I was being an optimist for sure.

Gary called on Monday and asked if I would like to go to dinner with him on Sunday evening. Sunday evening? That was different. Sweet Tomatoes? I never had a date at Sweet Tomatoes before, that would be different too, I realized.

Remember, keep your distance, I practiced, as I walked towards the entrance of the restaurant. You want to get to know him really well before you fall for him and, besides, he's got three kids.

There was no sign of Gary as I stepped up to the door, but as I glanced beyond to the bench nearby, I saw him sitting, in shorts. *Shorts? That was a first. I was used to guys dressing up for me. Who was this guy?*

We had casual conversation during dinner. He told me about his kids. I told him about mine. I found out he was in the printing industry. I told him about my teaching, and classes I was taking. I examined him more closely while we talked. Nice eyes, I thought. They are really pretty blue, with dark curly eyelashes. I really liked that. Nice skin too, smooth. I liked that too. His hands were gentle. I could tell by looking at them. Wavy, silver hair, that was nice too. Not too tall, that was OK. I preferred to be more eye-level anyway.

After we were finished eating, we parted our ways. That's weird, I thought. I was used to guys who wanted to hang out as long as they could. No sparks were flying, but *there was something about him. I was intrigued.*

A few days later, I got a card in the mail. I opened it. It was from Gary. Inside it said:

Wanna Karaoke?

He'd really listened to me. I told him I loved to sing karaoke. I was impressed indeed.

I couldn't wait to see what else he had up his sleeve.

CHAPTER 32

OPENING MY VOICE

I t was the fall of 2002.

Gary and I continued to spend time together. I kept some distance and continued dating other men at the same time. With the time we spent with our children, we saw each other only a couple of times a month. I still wrestled with myself, but there was something about his kiss that kept me coming back for more. *I don't think I'd ever kissed anyone where it felt so natural.* We found that we did have a lot of chemistry together too. I guess I was just scared. Those old demons were creeping in to make me stuck at times.

We were at dinner. This time it was El Torrito's. We were in a cozy corner booth that lent itself to intimate conversation. We were both risking deeper conversation than where we had gone to this point. I decided it was time to push it further to see if there really were more possibilities that existed between us. I think he wanted to know if I could be more present for him, with my distance and noncommittal responses to him.

"So what are you looking for in a relationship?" I questioned him.

"I really want emotional intimacy," he replied.

I looked back deeply at him. *Was he for real?* If men are from Mars, he must be from some other planet. "Really?" I asked.

"Yes, it's one of the things at the top of my list, next to family and God," he said.

"That's unusual for a man," I commented.

"I don't think so, isn't that something that many of us want and need as humans, to have someone close to us who accepts and embraces us?" he elaborated.

"Well, I know I want that, I didn't think men thought like that." I explained. *Wow, he's much deeper than I realized. I knew there were reasons I was sticking around. He's different than other guys.*

"Carrie, I have a question for you," he asked tentatively.

"What's that?" I queried.

"I bought some drums a while back because I was in a band in middle school and high school. I've been practicing so that I could teach myself to play again. It would be so cool to be part of a group. I would love that. So, I was talking to a co-worker the other day about it and found out he and his wife were in a rock band in Canada," he spewed excitedly.

"Really?" I responded.

"Yes, and he wants me to come play drums with them. He plays guitar and his wife sings. Would you like to come too, and you could sing with his wife?" He looked my way with hopeful eyes.

'That sounds like fun! When would it be?" I probed.

"I'm shifting my schedule with the kids so you and I can spend more time together. We could go to Sacramento, where their house is, on the weekend when we don't have our kids," he further explained.

I loved to sing, and he knew it. Well, he definitely had my attention now.

Two weeks later, we were on the drive to Sacramento. We had lots of time to talk and get to know each other better when we were en route. I found out he was from South Carolina. He had grown up with three sisters. His dad died when he was seven. I empathized with him. His dad was an aeronautical engineer. Gary must be very smart too, I thought.

He spoke passionately about his family, his mom and stepdad, and his children. I could see that he was a dedicated father and from what I had learned, seemed to be of high integrity. I was beginning to see who the core of him was. This is so much better than the facades of men I had met at dances, I thought. Gary is the real deal, and to think I met him at the grocery store. I laughed.

"What's so funny?" he asked.

"Oh nothing," I lied. I was really laughing because I was thinking, instead of shopping for groceries, little did I know I was shopping for a man, that day in June.

At Carl and Rena's we unloaded Gary's drums and placed them into the designated space. Rena was very friendly, as was Carl. It felt like we'd known them for a long time already. It didn't take long to see that they were very serious about their music. They shared a video showing them playing for an enormous crowd of people in Canada. Turns out, they were rock stars.

It's going to be tough measuring up. I had always loved music, and played piano and guitar myself. I hadn't played at a professional level, but rather, mostly for personal enjoyment. I would play the piano at church sometimes, but less often it seemed, since becoming a single parent. I admitted my inadequacies.

Rena immediately disagreed, "You have a beautiful voice, you just need to sing out. Open up your throat."

Open up my throat? I thought I was opening up my throat, I moaned internally.

"Look, like this," as she demonstrated one of the many ways she instructed me to move my mouth. She showed me how to drop my chin too. She also encouraged me to sing forward to make a fuller, more solid sound. It was hard work. I was being stretched and challenged in ways I wasn't used to.

"Carrie, take a pencil and push it crosswise in the back of your mouth while it is open, and then sing runs up and down. It will open up your throat. Trust me," she continued instructing me.

"I'll try it next week," I agreed.

We continued to meet Rena and Carl every month for at least nine months. We had lots of fun. We laughed while we created all kinds of different sounds and songs together. We began focusing on songs that we felt worked best for us as a group.

"Carrie and Gary, how would you like to record our music?" Carl suggested.

"You can do that?" we chimed in together.

"Yes, didn't we show you our studio?" Rena asked.

"No," I offered.

"I think Carl mentioned it to me at work," Gary remembered.

"Next time we get together, let's plan on recording the songs and making a CD," Rena offered.

I was excited. I had never made a CD before. Rena had been so sweet to give me on-going lessons during our get-togethers. I could feel my voice opening up and getting stronger. I have to admit, I no longer recognized the sounds that came out of me when I was singing. I was no longer familiar with myself. I always had such a soft, reserved voice, and now it was being recreated.

Gary and I were getting closer too. The holidays had passed and we were spending time with each other in a more committed relationship. I noticed that he had a lot of other friends too, who respected him as much as Carl and Rena. Gary wasn't afraid to put himself out there. *I could learn from that.*

He was always so accepting and encouraging too. I really appreciated that and could feel myself being more comfortable with him, and the possibility of a future together.

We were once again on our way to Sacramento. This time our trip would culminate in the making of our CD. I could tell Gary was just as excited as I was. This is fun, I thought. When we arrived, Carl and Rena were in the back room setting up. Rena opened a closet and revealed her floor to ceiling collection of music. Wow, I thought, a lifetime of music.

When it was my turn to sing, I put on the headphones and leaned towards the microphone. Just like in the movies, I mused.

"Don't be afraid to open up and drop your chin down," Carl reminded me.

"I will do my best," I responded back.

I could feel Gary watching me, with pride. *I hoped I wouldn't disappoint him.*

When I opened my mouth to sing, the sound came right back to me in the headphones. *That's really me.* I was pleased beyond words. It really was a big, open, clear sound that came from my voice. Miles from where I had been nine months earlier.

I looked over at Gary again. He was beaming, that full-mouth wide grin of his, the same one from the grocery store. Could Gary be partly responsible for who I was becoming?

Then it hit me, *as my heart had been opening up, so was my voice.* He really did have something to do with it.

Thank you Gary. Thank you Rena and Carl. Thank you, God.

CHAPTER 33

CAUGHT BY SURPRISE

The air was thick with the smell of sunscreen and sea salt, on this island paradise far from home.

Erin, Kayla and I were in Hawaii enjoying a free five day, four night stay, thanks to one of my timeshare gifts. I had no intention of letting it go to waste. It also gave me the luxury of sharing this generous trip, that I might otherwise have felt I could not afford.

What started as a free trip on July 12, 2007, turned out to be a very expensive venture.

We had just unloaded our suitcases in the hotel room. The girls did not even try to hide their disappointment. The scantily furnished room definitely did not hold the promise of resort indulgences. The beds were flat and stiff looking, without even a hint of soft cushioning underneath the bland yellow spreads that were their covering.

Further glances told me that the room disclosed no separation either. Oh no, I thought, it's going to be tough getting them to go to sleep at bedtime. With one television and the lack of a sofa to widen the room for variances in lighting, there would be little hope of reconciling differences that would surely reveal themselves in the evening light. I put on a big smile and thought, we'll have to make the best of it.

The girls, however, were not so quick to reconcile themselves to a five-day stay in this meager room. *Why had I thought it would be more resort-like?* I tossed around in my head. *Guess I should have known better, it was free, after all.*

I did not want to let that ruin this rare opportunity to share time with the girls in paradise.

At least Hawaii is often thought of as a paradise. The sweat developing under my arms from the humidity made me wonder who coined that term. After we got our things settled, we decided to go outside exploring.

We discovered the beach a short ways up the road. The girls were anxious to put their feet into the ocean and test out the sand beneath their toes. It looked awfully crowded to me, but I went along for the ride. *I want them to have fun,* was my thinking. Numerous surf boards were tilted up against the stand next to the outdoor restaurant we walked past. Nearby were the tanned, sleek bodies that went with them.

It was OK to look, right? The girls noticed too, as I watched their eyes wandering. *Better keep a close eye on them,* I reminded myself. The wind picked up a hefty speed as we meandered along the edge of the water. I wondered if it was always this windy. Dusk was settling in and my stomach began beckoning to be fed. The girls started to feel it too.

We sauntered underneath the grass overhang of the outdoor restaurant where they had already lit tiki lamps to warm the eating area. We sat down and browsed the menu for the choices that were available. *Lots of tropical fruit dishes, I love it,* ran through my mind. The prices, however, I did not love. My memory searched its banks to try and discern whether the hotel room had a refrigerator. *Don't want to waste any of this food,* I thought.

Erin chose an exotic fish and salad dish. Kayla went for the hamburger.

"Kayla, you mean you have all these wonderful choices and you only want a hamburger?" I pressed her.

"Yes, I don't want anything new," she responded.

I opted for a main dish salad, with lots of colorful and interesting garnishes.

I looked at the girls as if seeing them for the first time. Erin was now almost twenty-one years old. She had just graduated from college with her degree in Biology. She married the summer before, when she was twenty. I felt badly that I could not pay for Alan, her husband, to join us. Kayla was sixteen and in high school. *Where had the time gone?*

They are both such beautiful girls. *I wonder if they know how really beautiful they are.* I pray for them every day that they are gaining the skills and strengths they need to be ready to face the world. It's so hard to let go. Erin is already becoming very independent and living away from home. Kayla will be there sooner than I know, I'm sure.

"So what should we do tomorrow?" I threw out.

"Let's spend the day at the beach," Kayla suggested.

"Or go shopping," added Erin.

"Just what I was thinking," I laughed.

On the way back to the hotel, we saw an outdoor market that caught our attention. We couldn't resist the allure of the smells of the pastries on display and the sounds of the flute music drifting past our ears. Oh what the heck, I resigned, we're on vacation. With that concession, we sauntered down the aisles checking out all the woodcarvings, brightly colored floral clothing items, and other attractive merchandise on parade.

"Look Mom, there's a Cheesecake Factory right next to our hotel," Erin pointed out.

Good, we won't have to walk as far tomorrow, I filed away in my mind. It looked like we would have lots of company, however, as there was quite a crowd waiting to get in.

The time continued to pass and I realized that we'd better get to bed. We made our way out of the maze and up the stairs to our room, located just across the street.

"So, did you get your fill of shopping?" I inquired.

"No, of course not Mom," they responded, with a worried look on their faces.

"Don't worry, I'm not done either," I acknowledged.

The task of getting ready for bed and settling in turned out to not be as challenging as I feared between the traveling, the warm sun, and long walks through the outdoor market.

The next morning I remembered that we had to attend the timeshare presentation that I promised, when accepting the free trip.

"Oh Mom," moaned the girls, "Do we have to?"

"No, you could hang out here until I get back if you want," I offered.

"I want to go with you," conceded Kayla.

"I'll go too," Erin chimed in.

A couple of hours at the most, and then we'll be on our way, I reminded myself.

"Cunningham," called the receptionist.

We made our way to the corner of the room where the salesman was waiting. I felt a little light-headed from the Motrin I was taking. Earlier in the spring I tore the rotator cuff in my shoulder and since then had been suffering tremendous pain. Seemed I lived on Motrin these days. I had just filled a new prescription a few days before our trip, which meant that I would be taking it during the entire trip. Oh well, it won't affect anything, I thought.

The experience that I'd gone through so many times before suddenly was a new experience with Erin and Kayla with me.

"Mom, look how beautiful that is," they remarked, during separate shots in the video, "it would be a lot more fun to stay in a place as nice as that," Erin added.

"Yea," agreed Kayla.

Uh-oh, perhaps this was not going to be the easy in and out appointment that I thought.

"Hey girls, ssh . . . try not to say too much when we're with the salesman, OK?" I suggested.

"Why?" Kayla questioned me.

"Because they will push harder for us to buy something and then we will be here a long time," I explained, "Don't you want to go to the beach and do other things?" I added.

"Yes, but why can't you buy this Mom?" Kayla pushed back.

"Yea, why not?" Erin added her voice.

"Because it costs too much money," I curtly responded.

The video was just ending and we were being lured into a separate room where our salesman, Henry, was waiting for us. He seemed nice enough, but they're all pretty much the same, I thought, always trying to make a sale.

"What brings you to Hawaii?" was his greeting.

"A free trip, and Erin's graduation from college," I chimed in.

"It's beautiful, isn't it?" he remarked. I had to agree.

The girls noticed the snack table and headed straight towards it. I followed behind to see what awaited us. "Sure, help yourself," Henry offered, "when you have what you want, join me at the back table."

We piled our plates high, knowing that it may be awhile before we could leave to get lunch. Perfect, I was thinking, so the girls won't get too restless.

"Have you been to presentations like this before?" asked Henry.

"Yes, lots of them," I honestly admitted.

"Do you like the idea of a timeshare?" he probed.

"Yes, it's just a matter of the expense," I confided, "as a single parent, I have to hang onto my money."

"I'm sure it's not easy," Henry empathized.

"So I won't waste your time, let me just tell you what we have to offer," he continued.

"OK," I agreed less than enthusiastically.

"Here in Hawaii we have a unique opportunity to offer more incentives for being part of a timeshare than other locations, because it's such a popular vacation spot," he boasted.

"Oh yea, like what?" My curiosity got the best of me.

"For one thing, when you purchase points you get 200,000 one time bonus points," Henry explained, "that can be used over the next three years," he added.

He continued explaining his offer, which included a discount card, free weekend getaway, and a VIP membership. The VIP membership apparently meant that we would have priority reservations available to us.

My foggy brain was having a hard time focusing. *What was wrong with me? Was it because I hadn't yet eaten a full lunch? Oh, maybe it's the Motrin.* I had been taking it for so long, I no longer clearly recognized its affects on me.

"Mom, let's do it," Kayla was clearly excited, by the sound of her voice.

"It would be fun, we could stay at much nicer places than the rank hotel we're in right now," Erin agreed.

"Ouch," I knew she was right, and I felt badly about it. I had wanted this trip to be so special for her graduation celebration.

"Girls, it's probably way too much money," rolled off my tongue, cueing Henry to slide into his next pitch.

"Let me show you the numbers. We make it really affordable," Henry continued.

He began speaking in a drone that became difficult to understand for my drugged-up brain.

I paid attention as best I could, and asked questions to try and absorb the details. I was very aware of the cheering section in the background. I swear I heard, "Go, Mom, Go," but I think I imagined it.

The words, well the payment won't be so bad, echoed in my brain. *Who was that? Was that coming from me?* Surely I wasn't thinking I could do this!

The next thing I knew, I had my signature floating on a dotted line, and a pile of books and forms stacked in front of me.

The salesmen from previous timeshare presentations finally had their sweet revenge.

I had finally said, "yes."

CHAPTER 34

THE AWAKENING

I t was back in the spring of 1997.

While reflecting on marriage in my small apartment, I understood that just as a marriage certificate is not what makes a marriage, a divorce decree is not what makes a divorce. The physical, spiritual, mental, and emotional union that is created between two people is what creates the marriage. The piece of paper is a public decree of that occurring, and the desire to "cement" it through time, to work to keep it that way through a commitment to each other. A divorce decree is a public announcement of what has already occurred as well, the physical, emotional, mental, and spiritual severing of the relationship between two people. It can be chosen, or it can result from the choices of one or both partners, so that it occurs as natural consequences for the relationship. What is of eternal importance is the sacred relationship between two people or the lack of it. What actually occurs in the relationship is what's most important and not what is reflected on a piece of paper.

I know now that this is what marriage is. It's not saying, "I do." It's not walking down the aisle. It's not saying words. But it's something that happens on a much deeper level between two souls that connects the fiber of their being and weaves their lives together in such a way that each becomes more whole, and more alive, and more vibrant than they could have become before. It's because of the tremendous love and nurturing that passes between them in the everyday acts of kindness out of the deep appreciation of the uniqueness of each person, that enables them to shine and to be in ways that they couldn't be on their own. I understand that now.

It's not that I believe in divorce any more than I did before. But I understand that we never really were married in many ways. We lived together, we walked down the aisle, and we said, "I do," but there was not a marriage of our spirits, of our beings, and of our lives, in the true sense.

Without my life experiences, maybe I wouldn't have had this understanding that I do now.

Perhaps I wouldn't have the deep appreciation of what's required to create it. Or, I wouldn't know the skills involved or be aware of the well-developed capacity to love another person, that a marriage requires.

So, I truly have been blessed.

Around this same time, I went to a meditation workshop. The facilitator asked us to bring to mind the one individual that had hurt us more than any other. I pictured Mark. She then asked us to think of a gift we could place into that individual's hand. Then, to think of what they would be placing back in ours. I thought of a butterfly's wing, for both of us. Butterflies are about transformation and new awareness. I think we each helped the other one to grow to love ourselves more.

I guess I have learned the things I was supposed to, just as they were meant to be. Maybe I made the best choices I knew how, each step along the way.

Fly, Butterfly, Fly . . .

CHAPTER 35

REFLECTIONS

Here I am in Angels Camp, California, at a resort, by myself. The air is pure, and the water fresh and clear. There is a peacefulness in the air that contributes to this, my writer's heaven, as I have spent the past week eating and sleeping with a pen in hand. Enya is singing in the background, and if I look out the window I can see picturesque green hills. I am fighting the urge to go outside and play in the warm sunshine. This story's already been too long in coming forth, however. It is April 7, 2010 and it's been thirteen years since we divorced. Kayla is now eighteen years old, and Erin twenty-four.

I am writing to you, the reader, in the hope that my story speaks to you in a way that brings healing to your own life. I've also written my story as a cathartic experience for myself to cleanse, and keep moving forward with my life, by speaking my truth. That's what it is, MY truth, not THE truth. The only truth I can share is my own, but I have learned that we must each find our own way in this life, so I encourage you to search out what is right for you.

In all honesty, I can't say it's been easy, whether married or single. There has been plenty of rough terrain for me to travail. I can say that now I am creating my own life and walking my own path.

After years of playing tug of war with Mark, we are finally able to lay the past to rest.

Below is an e-mail he sent to me on February 14, 2010:

Hello Carrie,

I wanted to let you know that I am a better man because of you being a strong woman. Because of your insistence to have children, I have two beautiful daughters in my life today. Because of you pushing me into grad school, I have more job options and make more money. Because of your suggestions of going into counseling, I was able to shed years of disbelief, low esteem and able to love myself for who I am. I just wanted to say thank you for those things and for seeing me through my illness.

I wish you and your new partner Gary, much happiness.

P.S. Please stop giving my name to the free vacation and condo seminars, I am not interested.

OK, so I hear you laughing right now. *Here I am, in a timeshare resort.*

This e-mail arrived like the grand prize on a game show, when I wasn't even a contestant.

Yes, we do have two beautiful daughters. Yes, I do have a new partner. He embraces me for who I am, and listens to me. He encourages me to create and explore those New Horizons which are beckoning me. He is committed to being with me, and is willing to do the work it takes to grow through conflicts and challenges. He accepts, and yes, loves me. And I am grateful.

Have I found joy? Yes, in those moments when I allow it to come forth. I find it in those times when I reach outside myself, to bless the life of someone near me. I find it in my close relationships. I find it in my children. I find it in nature and all its glory. And I find it in this moment, when I feel I am fulfilling my purpose in sharing my story. Sometimes the surges of joy pulsate through me, and I need to dance or sing to let it out. I keep thinking this is probably going to end pretty soon, but it doesn't. The surges keep coming, even though it's been years now since I've been on this new path. So I hope to stay connected with the life force that continues to pour through me and to bring me joy.

May you be blessed with much of the same.

In peace and love,

Carrie

EPILOGUE

NEW HORIZONS

A new vision enthralls me. A flag, with five intertwined rings in the center, waves in all its victorious glory. Four rings represent the mental, emotional, physical, and spiritual dimensions of the self. The fifth ring represents the unconscious and conscious interplay that weaves these dimensions together in our everyday lives. I think that's where God is. It is the center ring on the top row. I am standing on the platform in front, with crowds of people sitting in the stands and cheering. The cheers are for all those that have been oppressed and awakened to transformation. There are many paths that have led us to this same destination. The applause is for me. My spirit reigns as buoyant as the eight year old's determination to remain afloat in the pool. I've surfaced. I just swam the butterfly stroke, the most difficult one of all. I am in the Olympics. The gold medal has been placed around my neck.

That image lingers, while I begin thinking about my car. A while back my car tried to get my attention. The temperature gauge moved into the hot zone. My nose told me that it was hot, as Kayla put it, we gave it "The Sniff Test." Instinctively I turned off the radio to listen for sounds that would give me clues for what might be wrong. I finally stopped for assistance. The mechanic found a compressed main radiator hose. He released the cap and then returned it, so that the hose could refill. It worked for a week or so.

My intuition told me that something else needed attention. When I went to shift the car into gear, it had the "feel" of something being wrong. I knew from past experience that it wasn't functioning properly. Because I'd also been stranded many times before, I had an "uh-oh" feeling in my gut. Sure enough, by 3 p.m. on the same day, the car had to be towed.

I had been receiving information from my car in all the possible ways I could. I think God tries to enlighten us with all the ways he has available to him to speak to us. Communication can come in the form of a voice or whisper, but it can also come to us through any kind of channel we have for understanding. It could be through dreams. It could be in nature, in a quiet kind of awareness. It could be in a sense of urgency, as a gentle, but firm tug to take action. It can be through another's voice speaking to us, as a powerful truth is quietly asserted. It can be through life experience. It can come as a sense of knowing, that we "feel" something to be right, or not right for us. The pathways leading to enlightenment are infinite.

My belief is that God is with us all the time. I also believe that we are all in this world doing the best we can. We make choices in each moment with the information we have at the time. We are not only a product of our upbringing and environment, but we each carry our own internal unique perspective. We interpret the events playing out around us in our everyday worlds. We live out our lives based upon those interpretations and the meaning we give to them.

That is one reason why forgiveness is so important. Forgiveness is removing the block that keeps love from flowing. It's how we love ourselves, by reminding us that we've not only done our best, but that others have as well. Without forgiveness we can't move forward to become all that we were meant to be. Each one of us is a miracle with our own personal destiny. When we are free and have truly forgiven ourselves as well as others, we can move forward to fulfill that destiny. It's my belief that we are here to not only learn and grow, but to share who we are and what we know to be true, with others, so they can learn and grow as well. Most importantly, as we allow forgiveness to flow freely, we can then reach out to others in love.

Isn't love what it's all about?

My mind takes me back to the meditation workshop. The question is, "What is your giftedness?" I ponder the question and realize that the answer has been sitting for a long time, waiting for me. My gift is in creating the heightened awareness of the beautiful and powerful spirit that resides in all of us. My gift is in assisting with building bridges of connection between people and within ourselves. My gift comes through my own awakening and transcendence out of the difficult circumstances of my own life.

My belief is that the greatest giving comes out of our own giftedness from the depths of our being. It is heart and soul giving, giving gifts that keep on giving. My gift is the message of hope and love that comes with the truth in knowing that we are all wonderful, beautiful, powerful beings with our own unique giftedness. What is yours?

As I have ventured into a new life, I have separated from the person whose song drowned out my own, and I have sought instead, the harmonious blending of song with another gentle spirit like myself. It's a path that I'm still walking, and still continues to lead me into even greater purpose as I share my life with a broader world in the hope that my experience will help to create New Horizons for others who have lost their way. And so, my friend, if you have been locked away in pain, I wish for you the New Horizons that can come from opening your heart to yourself, to others, and to the world around you.

Because of my unique life experience, the one affirmation I've learned to carry with me is this:

In every situation, I find I can re-claim myself and my worth.
I hold onto the thought—this too shall not de-value or lessen me.

ABOUT THE AUTHOR

Carrie Cunningham has held positions as a special education teacher, school counselor, and regular classroom teacher for the past thirty-three years. She has served as a Priest and an Elder in her church. She holds a master's degree in Guidance and Counseling from California State Fresno, and has obtained both the Mild/Moderate Specialist Credential and Multiple Subjects Credential in the state of California. She has conducted, instructed, and participated in numerous community workshops and trainings for adults, including counseling and spiritual growth topics.

Her daughter Erin graduated from medical school and is working as a PA in a pediatric clinic. Kayla is completing her BA degree and continuing her education to become a therapist. Carrie enjoys spending time with her daughters. She also enjoys writing music, attending fairs and festivals, traveling, reading, and the outdoors.

Carrie is passionate about telling her story. She is available to engage in interviews and speak to groups that need her message. She is well respected, and easily approachable. She and Gary, her companion, live in the San Francisco Bay Area.

Her e-mail is: carrieoasis@gmail.com.